Following God

Joseph

BEYOND THE COAT OF MANY COLORS

Following God

Joseph

BEYOND THE COAT OF MANY COLORS

MARY ENGLUND MURPHY

Advancing the Ministries of the Gospel

 **AMG** *Publishers*

God's Word to you is our highest calling.

Following God

JOSEPH: BEYOND THE COAT OF MANY COLORS

© 2011 by Mary Englund Murphy

Published by AMG Publishers. All Rights Reserved.

First Printing, 2011

ISBN: 978-0-89957-333-5

Editing by Rich Cairnes and Rick Steele
Layout by Jennifer Ross and Rick Steele
Cover design by Michael Largent at Indoor Graphics, Chattanooga, Tennessee

Printed in Canada
16 15 14 13 12 11 –T– 6 5 4 3 2 1

I dedicate this book to:

Sharon Clark

My dear friend who
loves Joseph almost as much as I do.
Thank you, Sharon, for helping make
this study a reality. And, to all those
living a Joseph life—you
know who you are!

Acknowledgments

There are so many people who encouraged me on my "caravan" that became this study of Joseph. Thanks to my family, especially my husband Bill, who was patient as I sat at my computer writing for many months.

A very special thanks to the late Dan Penwell. If it had not been for Dan I would have stopped writing before I began. He encouraged me at my first writers' conference, introduced me to his lovely wife, Gloria, and they became my dear friends and mentors. Gloria read as I wrote, and I'm so grateful.

Jeannie St. John Taylor read every word I wrote (sometimes twice) and talked to me on the phone nearly every day for months (years?). Jeannie kept me going when I wanted to quit. I love you, Jeannie!

Rick Steele believed in Joseph from the first time I pitched the idea to him at a writers' conference. Thank you, Rick, for helping me make Joseph a reality.

MARY ENGLUND MURPHY

About the Author

Mary Englund Murphy is the founder of Looking Glass Ministries and the author of the book *Winning the Battle of the Bulge: It's Not Just About the Weight* and the companion workbook/journal *Planning for the Battle of the Bulge.*

Mary believes every Christian can reflect Christ's love and live a full and abundant life regardless of past circumstances. Having survived cancer as an infant, being raised in a blended family, experiencing the death of her sister at an early age, and overcoming other devastating childhood events, Mary has learned to turn tragedy into triumph through Christ. Her passion is to use her life story to give hope and direction to those who are bound by past regrets.

Mary and her husband Bill have been in ministry for over thirty years and have three grown children Rachel, David, and Jonathan. They reside in Tulsa, Oklahoma, where Bill is the senior pastor of Calvary Bible Church (cbctulsa.com).

She attended Florida Bible College and has worked as a pre-school teacher, a personality profile writer, and grant writer. She has written and taught Bible studies and helped organize and lead youth camps and women's retreats. Mary is a graduate of the CLASServices speaking seminar and speaks for retreats, conferences and other special events. Mary is also a member of the Advanced Writers and Speakers Association.

About the Following God Series

Three authors and fellow ministers, Wayne Barber, Eddie Rasnake, and Rick Shepherd, teamed up in 1998 to write a character-based Bible study for AMG Publishers. Their collaboration developed into the title, *Life Principles from the Old Testament.* Since 1998 these same authors and AMG Publishers have produced six more **character-based** studies—each consisting of twelve lessons geared around a five-day study of a particular Bible personality. In 2001, AMG Publishers launched a series of topical studies called the **Following God™ Discipleship Series.** Soon after, books were released in the Following God™ **Christian Living Series,** which is also topical in nature. Though new studies and authors are being introduced, the interactive study format that readers have come to love remains constant with each new Following God™ release. As new titles and categories are being planned, our focus remains the same: to provide excellent Bible study materials that point people to God's Word in ways that allow them to apply truths to their own lives. More information on this groundbreaking series can be found on the following web page:

www.amgpublishers.com

Preface

If you grew up attending Sunday school, vacation Bible school, or any kind of Bible training, chances are you know something about Joseph of the Old Testament. Or, perhaps the sum of your knowledge is drawn from Andrew Lloyd Webber's *Joseph and the Amazing Technicolor Dreamcoat*. Whether you know Joseph well, or you've never heard of him at all, you're in for eight weeks of adventure!

Joseph's life is typically viewed from an overall perspective—the favored son, the dreamer, the betrayed slave, the prisoner, the vizier of Egypt; a man who was loyal, faithful, worshipful, and honest. There it is—Joseph in a nutshell. But for many of us, the story is so familiar we often see the shell but miss the nut, for it is so much more than a simple Sunday school account or a coloring paper of a young boy in a striped robe.

It's true, Joseph was blessed with power, wealth, children, and prestige, but that's the end of his story, Anyone could be faithful to God with all that, right? But remember, when his trials began, Joseph didn't know the end of his story any more than you or I know the end of ours. He was a man who lived a life of faithfulness, never knowing what the future held. During his first thirteen years in Egypt he was betrayed, shamed, and forgotten, and had no idea he would someday rise to one of the most powerful positions in the world.

Aside from Jesus, Joseph has come to be my favorite biblical character. In fact, I would say I have a passion for Joseph's life. Perhaps it's because I can relate in so many aspects. Like him, I was born into a blended family; I have had twenty-one half-, step-, and adopted brothers and sisters, two stepmothers, and three stepfathers. I have been the favored child, and at times the ignored and lonely child. I've been despised and wrongly accused by members of my family, and I have been suddenly moved to an unfamiliar town where I didn't want to live.

But Joseph's story isn't just for me. The more I study, the more I realize his life gives practical application, hope, and direction for everyone. My prayer is that you will see Joseph with a fresh insight. Put aside your preconceived ideas and see Joseph's life through his very eyes—the lonely little boy ignored by his brothers, yet coddled by his parents. Join him in the terrifying pit, follow his caravan to Egypt, and stand with him on the slave auction block. Feel his struggle for purity, go with him to the dungeons of Egypt, and rejoice in his rise to power. Most of all, identify your own lives with his as we learn to live a life of grace and forgiveness.

My prayer is that God would speak to you through His Word every day and that you will gain new and practical insights. As you look at passages that are perhaps very familiar, ask Him to show you truths you may have overlooked. Begin each day's lesson with this prayer from Psalm 119:18: *"Open my eyes, that I may behold Wonderful things from Your law."* In a few days, you'll know it by heart!

MARY ENGLUND MURPHY

Table of Contents

1

You Don't Get to Choose Your Family

Have you ever wished you were born to different parents? Have you longed for the normalcy that seems to be part of every family except yours? Oh, to be part of an ordinary family! As I've lamented over certain aspects of my own childhood, and observed other families, I've come to the conclusion there are few, if any, that are ordinary. Each has its embarrassing relatives, closeted secrets, and set of idiosyncrasies and problems.

In the past few decades, terms such as *blended* and *dysfunctional* have been coined to describe complex family relationships. As you will soon see, Joseph's family gives an entirely new dimension to both these terms. Yet, to get a complete picture, it's important to look beyond his immediate relations and examine his ancestry. His lineage consisted of such Bible luminaries as great-grandparents Abraham and Sarah, grandparents Isaac and Rebecca, and parents Jacob and Rachel. With a family tree like that, who could have problems with relatives, right? Wrong!

One of the wonderful things about the Bible is that it records the good, the bad, and the ugly, and that is certainly the case with Joseph's family. As we study his incredible life we will see how he and his brothers were directly affected by the decisions and actions of their forefathers, but how each made vastly different choices.

ABRAHAM AND SARAH: INTEGRITY MATTERS

Pray this verse: *"Open my eyes, that I may behold Wonderful things from Your law."* (Psalm 119:18)

Have you ever tried to help God out—you know, by saying just the right words to sway someone to your point of view or trying to arrange circumstances so things will work out according to your plan? Have you ever stretched the facts or artfully sidestepped an issue to avoid facing an unpleasant situation? I tried to word those questions tactfully but the actual terms might be better expressed as "controlling, manipulative, or deceitful." Ouch! I think it's safe to say we've all been there at one time or another, and today we'll see that Abraham and Sarah struggled with the same problems.

Abraham and Sarah (originally known as Abram and Sarai) are considered persons of great faith, yet at times their faith appeared nonexistent. I don't know about you, but that could very well be me. One day I'm trusting God completely and the next I'm fretting and worrying. I'd like to think that if I had physical encounters and verbal conversations with God, as Abraham and Sarah did, that my faith would never again waver and I would always act in obedience. Sadly, I would probably respond just as they did. But in spite of their ups and downs God used this couple mightily.

📖 Read Genesis 12:1–3. List the seven elements of God's promises to Abraham.

_____

_____

_____

_____

God told Abram to leave his father's house and go to a new country. There the Lord would make him into a great nation, bless him, make his name great, make him a blessing, bless those who blessed him, curse those who cursed him, and bless all the families of the earth through him. Can you imagine? God identifies Himself, speaks to you, lays out His plan, and gives you His word. You just have to wait as He fulfills those promises. Could anything be simpler?

Abram was seventy-five years old, childless, and married to a sixty-five-year-old barren woman. Although life expectancy was longer in Abram's day, I'm sure he wondered why God was waiting so long to start fulfilling His promises. How would God make a great nation through him? When would the babies start to come? Ah! But God delights in working through us when all seems impossible.

Sometime after the Lord spoke those promises, Abram and Sarai, along with their nephew Lot, servants, and flocks, sought temporary relief in Egypt from a famine. Here Abram faced a test of faith.

God changed the names of Abram (meaning "high father") to Abraham (meaning "father of a multitude") and Sarai to Sarah (both mean "princess") when He confirmed His covenant with Abraham (Genesis 17).

📖 Read Genesis 12:10–20.

What was Abram's fear?

_____

_____

_____

How did he propose to solve his problem?

_____

_____

_____

What was faulty about Abram's reasoning?

_____

_____

_____

How did Abram's sin affect Pharaoh's household?

_____

_____

_____

📖 *Doctrine*

THE ABRAHAMIC COVENANT

God formalized His promises to Abraham through the Abrahamic covenant (Genesis 15). He confirmed the promises in Genesis 13:14–18; 17:1–27; 18:1–18; 22:1–19; 26:23–25; 35:9–15.

How quickly Abram resorted to deceit when his faith was tested! Instead of turning to God for guidance and protection when faced with a seemingly perilous dilemma, he tried to manipulate people and circumstances. God had promised to make him a great nation and bless the world through his descendants, yet Abram jumped to the conclusion the Egyptians would kill him in order to take Sarai. He deceived the Egyptians by presenting her as his sister rather than his wife. Using his God-given authority as head of the home, he carried out his deception, and no doubt included his nephew and servants in the scheme. Instead of placing complete trust in God's promises, he was in fear and took the coward's way out.

Some say Abram didn't really lie because Sarai was his half-sister (Genesis 20:11, 12), so it was simply a half-truth; after all, he couldn't help what others believed. No! Abram's *intent* was to give the wrong impression by presenting truth in a misleading way; he purposed to deceive, and God holds us accountable not only for our words and actions, but our intentions as well: *"For the word of God is living and active . . . it judges the thoughts and attitudes ["intentions" NASB] of the heart. Nothing in all creation is hidden from God's sight. Everything is uncovered and laid bare before the eyes of him to whom we must give account"* (Hebrews 4:12, 13 NIV).

Pharaoh was so delighted with Sarai he rewarded Abram with gifts of livestock and servants. While Abram profited from his deception, God inflicted plagues on the Egyptians. No doubt Abram thought it was just a small deceit, but sin always affects those around us and often has far-reaching and long-lasting consequences. God will not be mocked, and we will suffer the consequences of sinful behavior (Galatians 6:7).

A half-truth is a whole lie.

Describe a time when your sinful attitude or choices affected others.

_____

_____

_____

_____

Word Study
LYING

The Hebrew word translated "lying" in Proverbs 6 (*sheqer*) means "untruth" or "sham." The word translated "lies" in this same chapter (*kazab*) means "to deceive."

📖 Read Proverbs 6:16–19 and Proverbs 12:22.

What is God's take on lying and deceit?

_____

_____

_____

How does God feel about those who are truthful?

_____

_____

_____

_____

How might the Lord have dealt with the Egyptians and Abram if he had been truthful?

_____

_____

_____

It's understandable Abram feared for his life, but it was wrong for him to deceive, for God always provides a way of escape in times of temptation (1 Corinthians 10:13). But, when lies and deceit become part of our personal and business practices, we show a lack of respect for ourselves and others. It exhibits a lack of faith that God can, and will, provide and protect. Unfortunately, half-truths, embellishments, and deceit have become the norm in our society. We make excuses for our sin and justify the means by which we achieve the solution we desire or think we deserve.

📖 Read John 8:32. What will set us free from a pattern of deceit?

_____

_____

📖 Read 1 John 1:9. What is the first step toward overcoming sin?

_____

_____

Abram wasn't alone in doubting the Lord's promises and questioning His timing. At seventy-five years of age, Sarai had given up hope of ever having a son and decided to assist God by supplying a solution of her own. Earlier we saw that Abram asked Sarai to unite in his deception, now we see she asked him to join in her lack of faith, and he quickly agreed to her plan. But, as so often happens, the results were disastrous.

📖 According to Genesis 16:1–3, what was Sarah's resolution to the problem?

_____

_____

_____

📖 Review Genesis 12:1–3. How does Sarah's solution contradict God's promise?

_____

_____

_____

God promised that an heir would be produced through Abram, thus including Sarai, not a concubine or second wife. Although other cultures accepted the practice of polygamy, it was never God's intent (Genesis 2:24). It appears that Abram's and Sarai's logic was "Everyone else is doing it; it must be okay." The standard for Christian behavior is not what everyone else does, rather what God asks of us in His Word.

📖 According to Genesis 16:4–16, what was the outcome of Sarai's manipulation?

_____

_____

_____

Beware when you try to manipulate people and circumstances to accomplish your agenda, and then pass it off as God's will. Sarai got what she wanted, but as soon as Hagar became pregnant, the tension between the two women became unbearable. To compound the problem, instead of taking personal responsibility, Sarai blamed Abram.

APPLY Can you think of a time when you lost hope in the promises of God and tried to influence others or manipulate circumstances rather than wait for God to work out the problem? What was the result?

_____

_____

_____

_____

Thirteen long years later, the Lord once again confirmed to Abraham and Sarah they would have a son.

📖 Read Genesis 18:1–15. How did Sarah respond when she heard the promise?

_____

_____

_____

> **The standard for Christian behavior is not what everyone else does, rather what God asks of us in His Word.**

What did she do when confronted with her response?

_____

_____

How quickly we deny or protest when we're caught doing something foolish or sinful! It isn't easy to admit we're wrong, but the Scriptures say we should humble ourselves before God and man (James 4:6; 1 Peter 5:6).

I wonder if there were times when Sarah thought she'd blown it—that there was no way God would bless her because of her disobedience. Sadly, that is what people sometimes think, but God is patient, gracious, merciful, and faithful to fulfill His promises in spite of our failings. One year later, when Sarah was ninety years old, she gave birth to Isaac, the son of promise.

Today we have focused on some of the shortcomings of Abraham and Sarah; in the weeks to come we will see how their poor decisions impacted future generations. But, in tomorrow's lesson, Abraham expresses the ultimate faith. In the years after Isaac was born to them, this incredible couple grew mightily and left a spiritual legacy of faith, worship, and obedience.

📖 Read 1 Peter 3:3–6. How is Sarah an example to the women of today?

_____

_____

_____

In what ways did God commend Abraham's and Sarah's faith in Hebrews 11:8–19?

_____

_____

_____

Hebrews 11 is considered the great faith chapter, and I think it's notable that more verses there are devoted to Abraham than any other single person.

APPLY Describe a time when you know God was working in your life and you demonstrated faith in Him.

_____

_____

_____

_____

_____

_____

Isaac and Rebekah: History Repeats Itself

Pray this verse: *"Open my eyes, that I may behold Wonderful things from Your law."* (Psalm 119:18)

At this point, one might wonder why God picked Abraham to be the father of His chosen people Israel, why He didn't give up on a man and a woman who lied, deceived, and manipulated and whose faith was erratic, at best. Well, it's because God is God—patient, loving, kind, gracious, forgiving; and, unlike us, He sees the end from the beginning. Just as He knew the end of Abraham's story, He knows the end of yours and mine, and He is trustworthy to carry us through to the finish.

In Philippians 1:3–6, of what is the apostle Paul confident?

_____

_____

_____

📖 Now read Genesis 22:1–19. Sounds like an adventure novel, doesn't it? Every time I read these verses I feel anxious anticipation, even though I know Isaac doesn't die. I can't fathom Abraham's faith as he followed God's command to offer up his son on the altar. Aside from Jesus, I can't think of anyone in Scripture who was faced with such a difficult test. My husband and I have been blessed with three wonderful children we dedicated to the Lord, but I don't know that I could do what Abraham did. He never hesitated to obey, nor did he withhold that which was most precious to him.

 Think about what is most important to you. Is it a person, a possession, your time, talent, finances, ministry, or job? Is there anything or anyone you are withholding from the Lord? What is causing you to resist releasing it to Him?

_____

_____

_____

_____

📖 Reread Genesis 22:4 and step into Abraham's sandals for a moment. For three days you travel, knowing at the end you're going to sacrifice your son on an altar—not just figuratively, but literally. This is your son of promise, the very son for whom you waited twenty-five years. Each step of the journey, each moment of the day, it's on your mind. No one in your party knows what is about to happen, because the agreement was between you and the Lord—even your son, the intended sacrifice, doesn't know.

What do you think Abraham and Isaac might have talked about during the journey?

> **"Being confident of this, that he who began a good work in you will carry it on to completion until the day of Christ Jesus."**
>
> **Philippians 1:6 (NIV)**

_____

_____

_____

We don't know what conversation was shared between father and son during those three days, but I believe Abraham reiterated to Isaac how faithful and awesome the Lord had been to him; how He had done the impossible by opening Sarah's womb when she was beyond the age of childbearing; how He forgave when they sinned. I believe Abraham repeated the seven promises given so many years before, reminding Isaac that he was the son through whom God would build a nation.

According to Hebrews 11:17–19, what gave Abraham the confidence to offer up Isaac as a sacrifice?

_____

_____

_____

Have you ever considered the fact that we have more substance on which to base our faith than Abraham did his? Think about it. Sure, Abraham had face-to-face encounters and verbal conversations with the Lord, but we have that evidence in addition to hundreds of other witnesses in the Scriptures, to say nothing of the modern-day testimonies of believers throughout the world. Perhaps we have even more reason to place our confidence in the promises of God than people at any other time in history.

Abraham believed God. It's that simple; he believed God was who He said He was, and that He would do what He said He would do. Abraham gave up trying to fix his own problems, and he finally got it: *"The word of the LORD came to Abram in a vision: 'Do not be afraid, Abram. I am your shield, your very great reward.' . . . Abram believed the LORD, and he credited it to him as righteousness"* (Genesis 15:1, 6 NIV).

I don't know what your present struggle is, but I do know that God will be faithful to get you through your most difficult crisis. Just as Abraham and Isaac faced their trial in faith, so can you.

Isaac—Son of Promise, Son of Miracles, Son of Sacrifice
Although Abraham's faith is generally the primary focus of this passage, it's essential to point out the tremendous faith of Isaac. We don't know his precise age but most scholars place him in his teens or early manhood. We do know he was old enough to understand what it meant to worship and sacrifice, and strong enough to carry a load of wood up a mountain.

Reread Genesis 22:6–10. What might Isaac have been thinking as he watched his father prepare for the sacrifice?

_____

_____

_____

What do you think went through Isaac's mind as he lay on the altar?

_____

_____

_____

It's significant that Isaac allowed his father to bind and place him on the altar, for he would have been strong enough to overpower a man of more than 110, or at the very least, he could have easily run away. Something stronger than a rope held Isaac in place. I believe that by the time he was bound on the altar, Isaac's faith was so firmly grounded he was prepared to obey God and his father without question, and that he, too, had absolute faith that God could raise him from the dead.

This was the heritage passed to Joseph and his brothers, and the kind we need to leave to our children—a legacy of the knowledge of God's faithfulness and unfailing love. Future generations need to know that God is trustworthy and deserves our praise, worship, and obedience. They need to know _they_ can trust Him with any problem, because _we_ are able to trust Him.

A Love Story: Isaac and Rebekah
After the death of Sarah, Abraham arranged for the marriage of Isaac and Rebekah, as was the custom of the day. It's a beautiful story of love, obedience, and faith on Abraham's part as well as that of his servant, of Rebekah, and of Isaac (Genesis 24). It is an affirmation of the unwavering faithfulness of our God, who listens and answers prayer.

If the story of Isaac and Rebekah were a fairy tale, we could end here and say they lived happily ever after, but it's an account of a real couple who made some poor choices along with the good. As a result, this marriage, too, had some struggles.

What promises did God confirm to Isaac in Genesis 26:1–5?

_____

_____

_____

What did Isaac do immediately afterward (vv. 6–10)?

_____

_____

_____

I want to yell, "Stop! Remember what happened to your parents? They told the same lie, and innocent people suffered. Don't do it! Choose truth, and the Lord will protect you!"

It's easy to judge Isaac and Rebekah, but we are often guilty of similar behavior; we commit the identical sins our parents did. How many times have you, or people you know, said, "I'll never do what my parents did; I'll never make the same mistakes they made"? And then, you watch in wonder as they (or you) tread the exact same path as the parents with the exact same results. I think we've all been guilty of that behavior. We don't learn from their mistakes, and we (and/or others) suffer the consequences. The Scriptures clearly state that future generations are impacted by both the good and bad actions of the parents (Exodus 20:4–6). Oh, that we would daily choose a legacy of truth, faith, and obedience, instead of dishonesty and deception!

President Harry Truman kept a sign on his desk that read, "The Buck Stops Here," meaning he had to take responsibility for the decisions he made; he couldn't blame others for the results of those choices. Generational sins can be stopped, and the "buck" must stop with us.

You Don't Get to Choose Your Family

DAY THREE

Where would you be if God lost His patience with you?

JACOB AND ESAU: O BROTHER, WHERE ART THOU?

Pray this verse: *"Open my eyes, that I may behold Wonderful things from Your law."* (Psalm 119:18)

Today we continue our look at Joseph's ancestry with the story of his father Jacob and his uncle Esau. We'll look at Scriptures that have been the subject of innumerable books, sermons, and Sunday school lessons. These accounts may be as familiar to you as they were to me, or you may be looking at them for the first time. As I prepared for today's study, I determined to view them with fresh eyes, and I hope you will, too.

📖 Read Genesis 25:19–21.

Isaac and Rebekah struggled with infertility for twenty years. How did they deal with it differently than Abraham and Sarah?

_____

_____

_____

What is more heartfelt and comforting than knowing that a loved one or friend has set aside their time to present our needs before the Almighty God of the universe?

Once again Isaac showed immense faith. He knew the promise: God would build a great nation through his offspring. But twenty years is a long time and, make no mistake, waiting for an heir was difficult for both Isaac and Rebekah. When we think of a childless couple the tendency is to focus on the wife's disappointment, yet husbands suffer, too. Isaac knew his wife endured the cultural stigma of infertility as well as the emotional ache of empty arms, but so did he. No doubt he longed for a child as much as Rebekah, and not just for the sake of passing on the covenant promise. But Isaac had learned one thing from his parents' experience. Instead of choosing a concubine or a second wife, as Abraham had done (and as his culture encouraged), he presented his request to the Lord, and I don't think he did it just once—I believe his prayers were ongoing.

Oh, to have someone share our pain, to know they are thinking of us! That's what Isaac did for Rebekah. What is more heartfelt and comforting than knowing that a loved one or friend has set aside their time to present our requests and needs before the Almighty God of the universe?

📖 Read Galatians 6:2. How did Isaac bear Rebekah's burden?

_____

_____

_____

_____

My husband and I struggled with infertility for several years. My heart broke the day my doctor said we would never have children. I tried to rejoice when my girlfriends became pregnant, but the news was always a bitter reminder I had no child of my own. We begged God for a baby; we consulted other doctors; we considered adoption. I don't know why God chose to eventually give us three children while some others have none, but I will never forget those who faithfully prayed with us, year after year.

APPLY Describe a time when someone interceded on your behalf and how the Lord answered the request.

_____

_____

_____

_____

📖 Read Genesis 25:22–26.

I can imagine how excited Rebekah was to finally be pregnant. But the babies were unusually active, and after waiting twenty years, she must have felt great anxiety, wondering if something was wrong. But she, too, went to the Lord in prayer. God told Rebekah the two sons within her represented two nations and the older son would serve the younger.

Based on the covenant promises God had made with Abraham (Genesis 15:1–21) and Isaac (Genesis 26:23–25), what do you think this message entailed?

_____

_____

_____

Dr. Henry Morris says, "Since one of the two must carry on the Messianic line and must inherit the promises of the Abrahamic covenant, it is crystal clear that God here told Rebekah that His covenant would be with the younger son, not the older."[1]

Certainly, Rebekah wouldn't keep a message this significant to herself; she would have told her husband. As head of the family, and custodian of the covenant promise of God, Isaac would be responsible to pass on the message to his sons. But subsequent events show a breakdown in communication and a return to deception and manipulation.

📖 Read Genesis 25:27, 28.

Isaac loved _____. Rebekah loved _____.

How might favoritism have contributed to a breakdown in communication?

_____

_____

_____

Why is partiality potentially devastating for any family?

_____

_____

_____

Describe a similar situation you've observed, perhaps even in your own family.

_____

_____

_____

It's imperative for parents to cultivate a bond of love and understanding with each child.

Although parents may naturally have a close relationship with the child who shares their mutual interests, and perhaps personality and temperament, it's imperative to cultivate a bond of love and understanding with each child. Isaac enjoyed eating the wild game Esau hunted, and their common interest created a special affection between the two men. Jacob, on the other hand, was a gentle, quiet man and found his work around the tents, developing a special bond with his mother. Clearly, Isaac and Rebekah did not have a balanced relationship with both sons. Their partiality produced a climate of jealousy and resentment as each sought to exalt the son they favored more.

📖 Read Genesis 25:29–34.

_____

_____

_____

Did You Know?
BIRTHRIGHT

Upon the father's death, the birthright included:

- a double portion of the inheritance
- the position of head of the family
- the position of spiritual leader of the family

The son (initially the eldest) who possessed the birthright in ancient times would receive a double portion, or share, of the inheritance and, upon his father's death, would become head of the household and serve as the spiritual leader. Although scholars differ as to whether the birthright was to be included with the blessing, ancient records show it could be sold. "Documents from the patriarchal era show that some actually did sell their birthrights, taking an immediate gain in place of a future inheritance."[2]

What did Esau value more than the birthright?

_____

_____

What was Esau's attitude toward the birthright (v. 34)?

_____

_____

Do you think Jacob tricked Esau into selling the birthright? Why or why not?

_____

_____

_____

The Hebrew word translated "despised" *(bazah)* in verse 34 means "to dis-esteem." In other words, the birthright held no value for Esau, and he read-ily sold it to Jacob for a simple bowl of stew. He was prepared to give up future blessings for a moment's pleasure. While we might criticize Esau's decision as rash, I wonder how many times we do essentially the same thing. We fail to value the blessings and rewards God has in store for us if we would only wait for His timing. We have adapted to our microwave culture; we want what we want, and we want it now!

APPLY Do you value the blessings and heritage that are part of your life? Can you think of anything you take for granted?

_____

_____

_____

Our next text is lengthy, but the content is so intriguing you'll hardly notice. Please read Genesis 27.

Can you believe it? Rebekah and Isaac knew that the Lord had chosen Jacob to receive the covenant blessing, yet Isaac tried to thwart God's plan and give the blessing to Esau, while Rebekah shrewdly foiled Isaac's plan so Jacob would get the blessing. And you thought your family had problems!

What is the guaranteed result of one's behavior found in Galatians 6:7?

_____

_____

_____

What appropriate action do you think Rebekah should have taken when she realized Isaac was going to bless Esau?

_____

_____

_____

More than seventy years had passed since God had spoken to Rebekah, but certainly, He had not changed His mind about who was to receive the bless-ing. Rebekah should have appealed to Isaac, reminding him God had cho-sen Jacob. Then, if Isaac was still set on giving the blessing to Esau, Rebekah should have put the matter into the Lord's hands and not used deceit to take what He was planning to freely give. We don't know how God would have worked out the problem, but she never gave Him the chance. Rebekah's actions revealed a lack of love and respect for her husband, for Esau, and for the Lord.

Rebekah did not need to take by deceit what God planned to freely give.

If Isaac and Rebekah had accepted God's choice of Jacob as the receiver of the covenant promise, and continued to teach and prepare their sons for His plan, this family would not have been fractured.

How might Esau's attitude have been different if he had been given an understanding that God had chosen Jacob to receive the birthright and covenant blessing?

_____

_____

_____

According to Genesis 27:41, what did Esau plan to do to Jacob?

_____

_____

What was Rebekah's solution to the problem?

_____

_____

Instead of coming together as a family to admit their faults, ask forgiveness, and try to reconcile, Esau harbored hatred and resentment toward his brother, Rebekah cunningly devised another plan, Jacob ran to escape conflict, and Isaac did nothing. The "modern" family have nothing on these folks!

I have a tendency to read biblical accounts and mentally critique the *should haves* and *shouldn't haves*. Abraham *shouldn't have* slept with Hagar; Sarah *should have* waited on God. Isaac *shouldn't have* tried to thwart God's plan; Rebekah *should have* trusted God for His outcome. Yes, they should have and they shouldn't have, but they didn't and they did, and in spite of it all, God was gracious and forgiving, and continued to work in their lives to accomplish His will.

We could make an endless list of should haves and shouldn't haves about our lives, too, but the great news is this: In spite of our past, He will use you and me when each of us turns back to Him!

APPLY Are you living in regrets of *should haves* and *shouldn't haves*? Confess your failings to the Lord and ask Him to use you to accomplish His will for your life. Don't let the past keep you from His promises and the future He holds for you.

_____

_____

_____

_____

_____

_____

Jacob, Leah, and Rachel: Two's Company, Three's a Crowd

Pray this verse: *"Open my eyes, that I may behold Wonderful things from Your law."* (Psalm 119:18)

Do you see patterns of behavior beginning to develop? We're only into the third generation of our study and have seen continuous failure to learn from parents' mistakes. Benjamin Franklin and Albert Einstein have both been quoted as saying, "The definition of insanity is doing the same thing over and over again and expecting different results." Of course, that's not the true definition, but it makes the point, and I get the feeling this family wanted different results even though they continued making the same unwise choices.

The next few chapters of Genesis are filled with accounts of unrequited and passionate love, polygamy, deception, reconciliation, deep sorrow and great joy, treachery, rape, incest, and mass slaughter. Certainly, no one can say the Bible is a boring book or that it only records the best of its characters. Those passages are fascinating to examine in detail, but today we'll focus on the associations between Jacob and his wives and father-in-law, and the emotional climate those relationships created for the entire family. (After the conclusion of our study, please read Genesis in its entirety; it's better than a page-turning novel.)

According to Genesis 27:41–46 what reason did Rebekah give Isaac for wanting Jacob to leave home?

_____

_____

_____

The Hebrew word for *flee* (barach) literally means "to bolt". What was the real reason Rebekah wanted Jacob to bolt to the safety of her brother Laban's home?

_____

_____

_____

No doubt Isaac and Rebekah desired that Jacob marry within the family clan, for Esau's Canaanite wives had been a source of irritation and disappointment. But Rebekah feared that Esau would kill Jacob and, instead of attempting to resolve the family conflict, she used a prospective wife for Jacob as an excuse to send him to safety. She felt that in time Esau's anger would subside and Jacob could return home. Sadly, Rebekah's interference and deception caused her to lose the very thing she longed for most—to have her favorite son by her side. By the time Jacob returned home more than twenty years later Rebekah had died and she never saw him again.

Why is it important to face conflict and seek to resolve it?

_____

_____

_____

APPLY Describe a time when unresolved differences in your family created lasting negative consequences.

_____

_____

_____

_____

📖 Please read Genesis 29:1–30.

How long did Jacob agree to work for Rachel's hand in marriage (v. 18)?

_____

_____

How did Laban trick Jacob (v. 23)?

_____

_____

Rachel's and Leah's roles in the scheme are unclear but you can be sure there were no happy participants the morning after the wedding. Jacob had waited for marriage until he was in his seventies, worked seven years, and then the love of his life was ripped from his grasp. What a way to start a marriage!

Try to picture the scene and the devastating wave of emotions when the deception was discovered. Describe how each person might have felt.

Jacob

_____

_____

Leah

_____

_____

Rachel

_____

_____

Laban

_____

_____

Brides in that culture were heavily veiled and the tents were dark. Though we have no specific details, the deception was easily accomplished.

Are you reminded of a verse from yesterday's lesson? Reread Galatians 6:7. How does it apply it to Jacob's situation?

_____

_____

_____

The irony can't be lost on anyone. Jacob obtained by deceit the covenant promise God wanted to freely give him, and now, deceived by Laban, he had entered into a covenant relationship with Leah and had physically consummated a marriage he did not want. No matter how much brotherly affection Jacob may have felt for Leah, he didn't want her for his wife. Laban, ever the conniver, offered Rachel (again!) to Jacob in exchange for another seven years of employment. Jacob accepted Laban's offer, and at the end of the customary bridal week for Leah, Jacob and Rachel were married, thereby entering into a polygamous relationship.

What alternate course of action could Jacob have chosen when faced with this difficult situation?

_____

_____

_____

Although polygamy was culturally acceptable, what was God's plan for marriage according to Genesis 2:20–24?

_____

_____

What potential problems do you see for the husband, wives, and children of a polygamous relationship?

_____

_____

APPLY Can you think of any behavior that has become socially acceptable in our culture in spite of being contrary to God's Word?

_____

_____

_____

There are those who excuse Jacob's decision to marry two wives because Laban had cheated him, and because polygamy was the norm for that culture. But life is not fair, and our choices and decisions should be based on biblical principles, not unfair or difficult circumstances. Cultural acceptability should not be the measuring stick for godly standards. I genuinely grieve for each of the parties involved; they were caught in a seemingly impossible predicament. Jacob had been cheated out of the wife promised to him; Leah was married to a man who didn't love or want her; Rachel wasn't just left standing at the altar—she didn't even make it to the altar!

The human inclination when facing a problem is to choose or create a solu-

> **Jacob obtained by deceit the covenant promise God wanted to freely give him, and then, deceived by Laban, he had entered into a covenant relationship (marriage) with Leah.**

tion that will make us happy, regardless of God's will, and that's exactly what Jacob did. But the troubles for this family were just beginning.

After each of the following verses note the issue that contributed to Jacob's marriage problems.

Genesis 29:16–18

_____

_____

Genesis 29:21–25

_____

_____

Genesis 29:28–30

_____

_____

Genesis 29:31–35

_____

_____

Genesis 30:1–5

_____

_____

Genesis 30:9–13

_____

_____

Genesis 30:14–16

_____

_____

Genesis 30:22–24

_____

_____

Genesis 33:1–2

_____

_____

Rachel held Jacob's heart, but Leah was able to produce the son-heirs Jacob desired.

Leah was jealous because Rachel was beautiful and loved by Jacob. Rachel was jealous because she was barren but Leah could have children. Life wasn't going according to their plans, and so they did exactly what their ancestors had done—they began to scheme, control, and manipulate circumstances and people to accomplish their desires. When they weren't able to bear children, they gave their handmaids to Jacob as concubines. Rachel and Leah passed Jacob from tent to tent and sadly, he didn't seem to mind. Within a period of approximately ten years, eleven sons and one daughter were born to Jacob and his two wives and two concubines.

Providing a loving, stable environment is difficult under the best of circumstances, but the marriage relationship lays the foundation, and creates the atmosphere into which children are born and in which they are raised. Children are uncannily perceptive of dissension and jealousies. They may not understand the particulars, but they can sense tension and disquiet. Death, divorce and remarriage, in-law interference, financial struggles, and other factors can adversely affect the emotional and spiritual growth of a child. Parents must endeavor to create an emotionally secure environment through which to pass down a godly heritage.

Rachel and Leah kept busy by acting out their jealousy and bitterness, Laban was preoccupied with establishing a secure economic future, and Jacob was seemingly oblivious, or at least passive, as the scene unfolded around him. While the actions of Jacob, Rachel, Leah, and Laban certainly made a profound impact on the children, just as significant were their attitudes. Bad behavior is simply a visible illustration of poor judgment, selfish ambition, and a negative mind-set. And while some have command over their outward behavior, if the attitude of the heart is wrong, others will eventually sense it.

According to Philippians 2:5, what kind of attitude should we have?

_____

_____

What does Ephesians 4:30–32 tell us to do with our bad attitudes?

_____

_____

You may be facing a trial in your life as potentially devastating to you as Jacob's was to him. You may be living with the wreckage of an ungodly heritage. I want to share a Scripture passage that I believe will comfort you when you can't see a way out of your problems:

> *Hear my cry, O God; listen to my prayer. From the ends of the earth I call to you, I call as my heart grows faint; lead me to the rock that is higher than I. For you have been my refuge, a strong tower against the foe. I long to dwell in your tent forever and take refuge in the shelter of your wings. Selah. For you have heard my vows, O God; you have given me the heritage of those who fear your name.* Psalm 61:1–5 (NIV)

Your family heritage may not be what you longed for, but you can be part of the heritage of those who fear the name of the Almighty God!

The marriage relationship is the foundation for and creates the atmosphere into which children are born and in which they are raised.

"For as he thinks within himself, so he is."

Proverbs 23:7a

Abraham's life is a reminder that God is faithful to keep His promises in spite of man's weaknesses.

FOR ME TO FOLLOW GOD

Pray this verse: *"Open my eyes, that I may behold Wonderful things from Your law."* (Psalm 119:18)

We've come to the end of our first week and I want to thank you for your diligence and participation as we've laid the foundation for our study on Joseph. I hope you've been able to gain new insights and have taken opportunities for some practical application. If you're reading about Abraham for the first time you may be surprised, even shocked, that God would make a covenant with a man who had such obvious failings and then continue to work through his descendants, many of whom also made poor choices. For those of you who know the story well, it's a reminder God is faithful to keep His promises in spite of man's weaknesses.

Do you remember the seven promises the Lord made to Abram in Genesis 12:1–3? Let's look back. God promised to:

1. Make Abram into a great nation.
2. Bless him.
3. Make his name great.
4. Make him a blessing.
5. Bless those who blessed him.
6. Curse those who cursed him.
7. Bless all the families (nations) of the earth through him.

📖 Read Galatians 3:6–9. Do you realize the Abrahamic covenant includes you if you have put your faith in Christ as your Savior? Look at the seventh promise again—God said *all* the families of the earth would be blessed through Abraham. That's you! The story of Abraham, Isaac, Jacob, and Joseph becomes your story, too, for you are a recipient of the covenant promise by faith.

Now look back to each of the main characters from this week's lessons. After each person's name, note at least one example of a *lack of faith* and one *act of faith* from his or her life.

Abraham
Lack of Faith

_____
_____

Act of Faith

_____
_____

Sarah
Lack of Faith

_____
_____

Act of Faith

_____

_____

Isaac
Lack of Faith

_____

_____

Act of Faith

_____

_____

Rebekah
Lack of Faith

_____

_____

Act of Faith

_____

_____

Jacob
Lack of Faith

_____

_____

Act of Faith

_____

_____

📖 I love the fact that even though the patriarchs had their struggles, God doesn't leave us with a negative image of them. Read Hebrews 11:8–21. In the spaces below, note the Lord's commendation for each of these heroes of faith.

Abraham

_____

_____

Sarah

_____

_____

Isaac

_____

_____

Jacob

_____

_____

Hebrews 12 likens our lives to a race, and adds a charge to believers to pursue a life of faith as did the men and women described in Hebrews 11. In order to follow God, we must lay aside anything that might weigh us down or cause us to lose focus. For some people that may mean pride, greed, anger, bitterness, addictions, selfish ambition, or wrong relationships.

📖 Read Hebrews 12:1–3.

Can you think of anything that is weighing you down in your race?

_____

_____

_____

What is preventing you from laying that aside?

_____

_____

_____

What tends to distract you and cause you to lose focus?

_____

_____

_____

How should we run our race?

_____

_____

On whom should we stay focused?

_____

_____

What will keep us from losing heart?

_____

_____

_____

"...let us run with endurance the race that is set before us, fixing our eyes on Jesus..."

(Hebrews 12:1–2)

This week we saw several instances in which our heroes didn't run an honorable race—they lied and/or deceived, blamed others, or tried to control and manipulate circumstances to their advantage. It's easy to take a self-righteous attitude and declare we would have acted differently given the same circumstances, but the truth is, we probably would be equally guilty. Search your heart as you answer the following questions:

Do you find it difficult to admit it when you're wrong?

_____

_____

Do you justify your actions or behavior?

_____

_____

Do you feel the need to control others?

_____

_____

Do you manipulate people or circumstances to achieve your goals?

_____

_____

Do you blame others rather than take responsibility for your actions?

_____

_____

Do you lie or in some other way deceive to get what you want or to make yourself look better?

_____

_____

King David of Israel could have answered yes to each of the previous questions. He committed adultery with Bathsheba, had her husband killed on the battlefield, and did all he could to cover up his sin, yet he is also credited in Hebrews 11 as a man of faith. Psalm 51 records David's prayer for forgiveness after his sin was discovered. If you answered yes to even one of the previous questions I would encourage you to read through his prayer and personalize it.

We've just begun to see the crazy, mixed-up family into which Joseph was born. All families experience conflict and frustrations; all families are dysfunctional in their own way; all families are subject to the effects of generational sin. But none of that gives us an excuse to continue in sinful choices. With God's help, conflict can be resolved, generational sin can be stopped, and the wounds from even the most horribly dysfunctional families can be

It's easy to take a self-righteous attitude and declare we would have acted differently given the same circumstances, but the truth is, we probably would be equally guilty.

With God's help, conflict can be resolved, generational sin can be stopped, and the wounds from even the most horribly dysfunctional families can be healed.

healed. The good news is that His grace is plentiful, as is His forgiveness, and He desires to accomplish His purpose in each of our lives.

 I pray that after completing this week's lessons you're able to see your own family circumstances in a new light. Answer the following questions as they specifically relate to your family.

Are you aware of any sins that have been repeated throughout the generations of your family?

_____

_____

_____

If so, what might you do to end the pattern and pass on a godly heritage to future generations?

_____

_____

_____

Do you feel that your parents showed preference to you or one of your siblings?

_____

_____

_____

How did that preferential treatment affect you?

_____

_____

_____

What new insights have you gained in regard to blended families?

_____

_____

_____

 Dear Lord, Thank You for the covenant promise You made with Abraham and for allowing us to be part of it through faith in Jesus Christ. I pray for those who have not yet accepted the blessing of the free gift of eternal life, and that their eyes would be opened. Thank You for the examples You've given us through the lives of Abraham, Isaac, and Jacob. Help us learn from both the positive and the negative, and to honor You with lives of integrity and character. I know there are no perfect families, and I want to consciously thank You for allowing me to be a part of my family. I pray You would help me recognize and put an end to generational patterns and sins; help me pass on a godly heritage to my children. In Jesus' name, Amen.

With your own family background in mind, write out a prayer of thanksgiving.

_____

_____

_____

_____

_____

_____

_____

_____

_____

_____

_____

_____

_____

_____

Works Cited

1. Henry M. Morris, *The Genesis Record* (Grand Rapids, MI: Baker Book House, 1979), 413.

2. Lawrence O. Richards, *The Bible Reader's Companion* (Owings Mills, MD: Halo Press, 1991), 40.

Notes

2

Taking Sibling Rivalry to New Heights

How would you like to be showered with love, attention, and gifts, and guaranteed a prominent position? Let's sweeten the deal and make you intelligent and physically attractive. That was Joseph's life, and though it sounds appealing, there were times when the reality wasn't so great. The special considerations given Joseph by his father caused intense sibling rivalry, and the entire family were affected by the results.

Through the conflict, Joseph conducted himself with godly character and uprightness. His brothers handled the problem in an entirely different manner: They didn't see an honorable way out, and their evil actions reflected their frustration. We can't blame the brothers for their *feelings*, but we can hold them accountable for their *actions*. They used circumstances as an excuse for sinful behavior, while Joseph chose to use his circumstances to make him a stronger person. They had the same models of faith and failure, and they had the choice which example to follow.

This week's lessons will include some of the more familiar aspects of Joseph's life, and I'm excited to get started. While most biblical narratives record portions of a person's adult life, in Joseph's case the Scriptures give insights and facts regarding his entire life—family background, birth, childhood, adolescence, young adulthood, employment, marriage, fatherhood, family relationships, and death. It's a fascinating study.

"A good name is to be more desired than great wealth."

Proverbs 22:1a

Did You Know?
NAME CHANGES

God changed the name of Abram to Abraham, Sarai to Sarah, and Jacob to Israel when He confirmed His covenant. Later, Joseph's name was changed to Zaphenath-paneah when he was promoted to vizier.

A Tale of Twelve Brothers: What's in a Name?

Pray this verse: *"Open my eyes, that I may behold Wonderful things from Your law."* (Psalm 119:18)

Some years ago, I saw a name in the obituaries that has stuck with me—Minnie Mickey Duckstein. Because names are a fundamental part of our identity, I couldn't help but wonder why her parents chose that name. Was she Jewish, as her surname might have indicated? Was she fun like her first and middle names? Did she ever think about changing it?

In our culture, we often name a child after a relative, friend, or celebrity, or just because we like the sound of a particular name. Some choose names based on ethnic heritage or create one entirely original. In biblical times, children were named for specific reasons. A name could reveal the parent's emotions or circumstances at the time of conception or birth, future hopes for the child or family, or even the spiritual relationship between God and the parents. Occasionally, a new name was given to an adult to reflect a change in status, position, or culture.

My husband and I chose our children's names not only because we liked them, but because they reflected something of our spiritual heritage. Our daughter Rachel (*ewe*) was a reminder Christ is the Lamb of God who died for us; David (*beloved*) was named after we had gone through a difficult trial and God had abundantly shown his love for us; Jonathan (*gift of God*) was so named because he was a welcome and unexpected gift.

Jacob's twelve sons and one daughter were named in the Hebrew tradition of identity and purpose. Each child (with the exception of Benjamin) was named by Leah or Rachel, and the names reflected their moods, desires, wounded or joyful hearts, and even feelings of vengeance.

Below is a list of Jacob's children according to birth order, identifying each one's mother and the Hebrew meaning of each name. In the spaces, note the emotional state of the mother and her rationale behind the naming of each child.

Leah, mother to:

• Reuben (*see you a son*), Genesis 29:31, 32

_____

_____

• Simeon (*hearing*), Genesis 29:33

_____

_____

• Levi (*attached*), Genesis 29:34

_____

_____

• Judah *(celebrated),* Genesis 29:35

_____

_____

Bilhah, handmaid of Rachel and mother to:
• Dan *(judge)*, Genesis 30:1–6

_____

_____

• Naphtali *(my wrestling)*, Genesis 30:7, 8

_____

_____

Zilpah, handmaid to Leah and mother to:
• Gad *(troop or fortune)*, Genesis 30:9–11

_____

_____

• Asher *(happy)*, Genesis 30:12, 13

_____

_____

Leah, mother to:
• Issachar *(he will bring a reward)*, Genesis 30:14–18

_____

_____

• Zebulun *(habitation)*, Genesis 30:19, 20

_____

_____

• Dinah *(justice)*, Genesis 30:21

_____

_____

Rachel, mother to:
• Joseph *(let him add)*, Genesis 30:22–24

_____

_____

• Benjamin *(son of the right hand)*, Genesis 35:16–18

_____

_____

Did You Know?

? JACOB'S CHILDREN

In order of birth:
- Reuben
- Simeon
- Levi
- Judah
- Dan
- Naphtali
- Gad
- Asher
- Issachar
- Zebulun
- Dinah
- Joseph
- Benjamin

Try to imagine what it was like growing up in Jacob's family—constant feelings of jealousy, envy, inadequacy, anger, and even triumph at outdoing one another. Yes, this blended family—one father, four mothers, and thirteen children—was definitely dysfunctional. And each time they were called by name it was a reminder that only one mother was passionately adored; that no matter how hard Joseph's brothers tried, there would never be equality in love and status; that one son would forever be favored above the rest.

What's in a Name?
If I introduced myself to you as Mary Englund Murphy, I would be telling you a little about myself. You would probably address me by my first name, Mary. My maiden name, Englund, would tell you of my father's Swedish heritage and that his religious background was likely Lutheran, and Murphy reflects my husband's Irish background. But unless I told you about my family history there's not much more you could learn from my name alone.

But such was not the case with Joseph and his brothers; their names identified them as individuals, a family, and a fledgling nation. They were the sons of Abraham, Isaac, and Jacob— the ones through whom the covenant promise would be passed down; the future heads of the twelve tribes of Israel; the beginning of the Jewish nation; God's chosen people. Their names reflected a rich heritage and a rich destiny.

The Hebrews, like other ancient cultures, were great storytellers, and children grew up listening to their parents relate the fascinating history of their people. Joseph and his brothers would have heard history all the way back to the creation of the world, including Adam and Eve and Noah and the great flood. But perhaps most thrilling of all would have been the stories how God made a covenant with their great-grandfather Abraham, and confirmed it with their grandfather Isaac and their father, Jacob. They would have heard both the favorable and unfavorable accounts of their forefathers, along with how the Lord's covenant love, faithfulness, and redemption were always evident. They must have wondered what part they would play in this promise to become a great nation, for the Abrahamic covenant was more than a story—it was their destiny.

Sadly, Joseph's brothers took on the identity of their given names and lived much of their lives as products of their environment and past. Joseph, however, took on the identity of his God and lived his life as a proud heir to God's promises, in spite of his circumstances. You and I also have a destiny designed by God especially for us. Founding a great nation as did Abraham or becoming vizier of a powerful kingdom as did Joseph may not be it, but God has a special plan for each of our lives.

The following Scripture passages were primarily written to the children of Israel, but they have a secondary application for us. Personalize each passage and note how it gives hope and encouragement for the plans God has for you.

Psalm 33:13–15

_____

_____

_____

Did You Know?

ISAAC

Isaac was still alive when Jacob's children were born. They probably heard stories of their heritage directly from him.

Isaiah 48:17

_____

_____

_____

Jeremiah 29:11–13

_____

_____

_____

 Are you living as a product of your past, or as an heir to the promises of God? Explain.

_____

_____

_____

"For I know the plans that I have for you," declares the LORD, "plans for welfare and not for calamity to give you a future and a hope."

Jeremiah 29:11

A New Identity and a Rich Destiny

When I was seven years old my parents divorced; my mother remarried a year later. Thereafter, on school days my mother had me use my stepfather's surname, but on weekends, when I was with my father, I went by my legal name. It was confusing for a young child and sometimes it was hard to remember which name I was supposed to use. I think it's fair to say I had an identity crisis. But when I by faith accepted Christ as my Savior I received a new identity as a child of God, and a new destiny—I was a Christian, a follower of Christ.

Perhaps you have suffered an identity crisis because of painful circumstances surrounding your name, reminders of a difficult past. Your family background may be as muddled as mine or Joseph's. It may be so appalling you don't even want to be associated with your family name; you may wish you had been born into a different family altogether.

The good news is we don't have to be a product of our past. When we trust Christ as our Savior we become children of God and heirs with Christ to everything God has to offer. Stop and think about what that means. _You_ are a child of the God of the universe.

Have you ever imagined what it would be like to inherit a fortune? I know I have. I've thought about the things I'd buy, the people I'd help, and the places I'd travel. I'll never inherit a lot of money—but I have an even immeasurably greater inheritance through Jesus Christ, and so do you. Your family may not leave you much of a tangible inheritance, either, but God gives all we need, and more.

After each verse below, describe the new identity and/or inheritance we have through Christ.

John 1:12

_____

_____

Word Study
CHRISTIAN

The Greek word translated "Christian" (Strong's #5546 definition in the _Key Word Study Bible_) is _Christianos_ (khris-tee-an-os) and means "follower of Christ."

Only if the storm accomplishes God's purposes, will He allow it to enter our lives.

Romans 8:16, 17

_____

_____

Galatians 3:26–29

_____

_____

Ephesians 1:18, 19

_____

_____

Ephesians 3:6

_____

_____

1 Peter 1:3, 4

_____

_____

We are all influenced by our background and environment, but that doesn't mean we have to become a product of our past.

APPLY How does knowing that you are an heir with Christ change your view of your destiny?

_____

_____

_____

Here's an assignment. This week, look up the meaning of your first and middle names, and find out if there were any special circumstances surrounding your birth and the choosing of your name. (You can find name meanings on the Internet.)

_____

_____

_____

Taking Sibling Rivalry to New Heights

DAY TWO

Joseph's Childhood: It Ain't Easy Bein' the Baby

Pray this verse: _"Open my eyes, that I may behold Wonderful things from Your law."_ (Psalm 119:18)

Raising children is difficult under the best of circumstances, but a brood of twelve children born over a ten-year period to four mothers (two of them sisters) and one father created unique challenges. It demanded exceptional parenting skills from Jacob, Leah, and Rachel, but sadly, they didn't always deliver. At times, Jacob passively ignored issues that called for decisive action, and Rachel and Leah seemed to spend more time trying to outdo one another than to create a stable, nurturing environment. Yes, Jacob's family was a unique blend, even by the standards of his day.

What struggles might the children have faced in this family setting?

_____

_____

_____

Compare Genesis 25:27, 28 and 37:3. What family error did Jacob repeat?

_____

_____

Jacob and Esau experienced firsthand the destructive effects of parental favoritism. It caused division between husband and wife, brother and brother, and parent and son. But Jacob showed partiality with his own children resulting in equally devastating consequences. He could not have been oblivious to the family turmoil he was helping create. He'd lived among jealous wives for years, and watched as they named their sons according to feelings of envy, bitterness, and vengeance. He knew Leah suffered from feeling unloved, and now he caused his sons to suffer, too. Certainly, he loved each child, but his obvious favoritism for Joseph created a breeding ground for resentment and ultimately hatred.

📖 Read Ephesians 6:4. How might Jacob's actions have provoked the other children to anger?

_____

_____

_____

Partiality is devastating, but especially so in a blended family. Children don't understand rejection, and they resent whatever comes between them and the object of their affection. As a result, they may lash out at the other children, or even the parent who is showing bias. The favored child is often shunned by the stepparent, who will try to make up for it by showing partiality to the other children. As a child from a blended family, I know from experience there are no winners when one child is shown preference. In *Great Expectations* Charles Dickens wrote, "In the little world in which children have their existence, whosoever brings them up, there is nothing so finely perceived and so finely felt, as injustice. It may be only small injustice that the child can be exposed to; but the child is small, and its world is small. . . ."

But you don't have to be a child to experience the emotional sting generated by favoritism, for it is equally wounding when a parent continues to

Jealousies would abound in any polygamous marriage, but try to imagine what it would be like for sisters to be married to the same man!

 **Word Study**
PROVOKE

The word translated "provoke" in Ephesians 6 (*parorgizo*) means "to anger alongside, enrage."

show partiality to a sibling in adulthood. Hurtful situations may also occur when a boss gives a raise to one employee but not to others, or in the church when leaders give recognition to some while others are overlooked—these are all settings for heartbreak. We humans are often unfair, but God is a God of justice, a defender of the oppressed, and shows no partiality, and He is the example we are to follow.

APPLY Describe a time when you felt you were unfairly treated by an authority figure.

_____

_____

_____

📖 Now read Psalms 9:9, 10; 56:11; 59:1, 2; 103:6.

After reading these passages, how do you feel about that situation now?

_____

_____

_____

"The LORD also will be a stronghold for the oppressed, A stronghold in times of trouble."

Psalm 9:9

We've reflected on those who have been victims of partiality and favoritism—but now consider the victimizer. As a parent, boss, church leader, or other authority figure, do you treat others fairly? Do you say or do things that provoke anger and resentment? If you're a parent in a blended family do you show favoritism to your own children above your stepchildren? Give an example.

_____

_____

_____

_____

APPLY If God is convicting you about exhibiting partiality, take action now to adjust your attitude and behavior. Ask God to show you the steps you need to take. Real change will require humility. List the people and/or areas where you need to make changes.

_____

_____

_____

_____

The Beloved Son
According to Genesis 37:3, why did Jacob love Joseph more than his other sons?

_____

_____

_____

Jacob loved Joseph because he was *"the son of his old age,"* but in truth, *all* the boys were sons of his old age. Jacob was in his seventies when he went to work for Laban, in his early eighties when he married Rachel and Leah, and ninety-one when Joseph was born. So what is the significance of *"his old age"*? I believe Jacob's love for Joseph was so great because he was the son for whom he had been waiting for nearly twenty years—the boy of his dreams. Joseph was the son and heir Jacob had envisioned fathering while he labored seven years for Rachel. Indeed, Joseph was the son he adored above all others because he was the child of the woman he adored above all others.

It wouldn't have taken long for Leah's sons to recognize that their mother was not the preferred wife or the best looking, and Bilhah's and Zilpah's sons would easily discern that their mothers, as concubines, were considered lesser. Children can be unkind under ordinary circumstances, but can you imagine the cruel name-calling as the boys took up defense of their mothers and their own full blood brothers? Put yourself in their place—life must have seemed pretty good until baby brother Joseph came along. Sure, there would have been some inequities, as in all families, but nothing compared with life after Joseph.

To make matters worse, Jacob wasn't subtle in his affection for Joseph or Rachel. After working for Laban for twenty years, Jacob returned home and sent a message ahead to Esau to apprise him of his arrival (Genesis 31–33). Fearful of his brother's reaction after twenty years, he arranged his wives and children in obvious order of increasing love and importance as they approached Esau and his men (Genesis 33:1, 2). Picture Jacob's entourage: animals and servants at the front, followed by the concubines and their sons, trailed by Leah and her children, and finally, Rachel and Joseph in the safest position at the rear. Even if the boys didn't initially comprehend the significance of the order at the time, in due course they would understand—their father loved Rachel and Joseph more, and he was willing to jeopardize the safety and well-being of the others in his family.

On the surface it would seem that Joseph was in the idyllic position among the children, but in reality, his childhood must have been quite painful and lonely. His brothers felt rejected by their father, and Joseph was, in turn, rejected by his brothers—everyone had reason to feel insecure. The sibling rivalry must have begun the moment Joseph was born, even before he understood what was happening. With whom did he play as a child? In whom did he confide his childhood secrets? No matter how hard he tried he would never be a part of their crowd.

And, to make matters worse, while Joseph was still young, Rachel died giving birth to Benjamin; the one person who really understood him was gone. Losing a parent at any age is difficult, but when that parent is not only your mother, but probably your best friend, it's even more devastating.

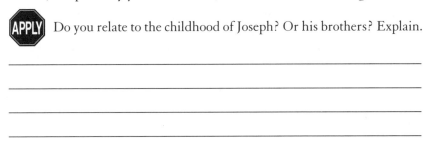 Do you relate to the childhood of Joseph? Or his brothers? Explain.

_____

_____

_____

_____

Put Yourself In Their Shoes
JACOB

Jacob was:

- in his seventies when he began working for Laban
- 91 when Joseph was born
- 108 when Joseph was sold into slavery
- 130 when he moved to Egypt
- 147 when he died

Jacob was willing to jeopardize the safety of the rest of his family to keep Rachel and Joseph from harm.

At the beginning of today's lesson, we focused on some of the negative aspects of Jacob's, Leah's, and Rachel's parenting, but it's important to remember they also exposed their children to a godly spiritual heritage. Between Genesis 32 and Genesis 35 Jacob begins to emerge as a spiritual leader, developing an intimate relationship with God. He twice meets the Lord, reconciles with his brother Esau, cleanses his house of foreign gods, builds altars of worship, has his name changed from *Jacob* ("heel catcher, supplanter") to *Israel* ("he will rule"), and the Abrahamic covenant is confirmed to him. Jacob was not always the ideal parent, but he was headed in the right direction—toward obedience and worship.

One might wonder how Jacob's sons could have been raised in the same family and turn out so different. They were all born into a dysfunctional, blended family, they all struggled with difficult childhoods, and they were all influenced by godly principles and instruction. Yet Joseph's heart responded in a way none of the other sons' did. Unlike his brothers, he somehow grasped and applied the concepts of godliness in spite of his upbringing.

We all have choices, and Jacob's children made vastly different ones. They could have learned from the negative behavior of their forefathers and made positive choices. Yet Joseph's ten brothers acted impulsively, made excuses for their bad choices, and blamed each other when faced with the consequences of their sin. There comes a time when we must take responsibility for our actions and accept the cost. We can no longer blame people, circumstances, location, finances, upbringing, or God.

You can't change your past, but you *can* use the experiences of your past to help you make wise choices for your future. Your beginnings may have been bumpy, but you can finish well. I believe Joseph made his choices to be faithful and serve God from the time he was a child, even though his own heritage was often lacking. He *chose* a life of obedience, character, and integrity.

Word Study
JACOB

The Hebrew name "Jacob" means "heel catcher" or "supplanter." God changed his name to "Israel," meaning "he will rule."

Taking Sibling Rivalry to New Heights

DAY THREE

Save time and avoid anguish learn from the mistakes of others.

THE COAT OF MANY COLORS: CLOTHES DON'T MAKE THE MAN

Pray this verse: *"Open my eyes, that I may behold Wonderful things from Your law."* (Psalm 119:18)

What's the first thing that comes to mind when you think about Joseph? Dreams? Slavery? Egypt? I think most people conjure up an image of that famous coat of many colors. Perhaps you colored a picture of it in Sunday school, or dressed your child in a multicolored bathrobe for a church pageant. For some of you this passage of Scripture is so well-known your mind virtually shuts down as you're hearing the story for what seems like the millionth time. Today, I want you to listen, *really listen*, to the story as if for the very first time.

But first let's take a little test. Whether or not you know the account well, try answering the following questions. No fair looking ahead!

Who gave the coat to Joseph?

_____

How old was Joseph when he received the coat?

_____

How was the coat different from other garments?

_____

_____

What do you think the coat represented to the family?

_____

_____

In your opinion, was Joseph a spoiled brat? Why or why not?

_____

_____

If you're like me, your view of Joseph has been greatly influenced by stories you heard in Sunday school and perhaps later as part of sermons in church. Even though I admired Joseph as an adult man of character, I saw him in his early years as a spoiled, self-centered child who flaunted the favoritism lavished on him by his father. But as I've read and studied the passages again, my position has changed. Let's examine the Scriptures together, and you decide for yourself.

Read Genesis 37:1–4. According to Genesis 37:2, while Joseph was working in the fields with his half brothers Dan, Naphtali, Gad, and Asher, he observed them behaving in such a way he felt compelled to tell his father. Was he being a tattletale as some Bible teachers contend? Was he purposely provoking his brothers, or was he being a wise steward and exhibiting loyalty to his father?

_____

_____

_____

As my husband and I raised our children, there were times they tried to get one another in trouble by tattling. Of course we discouraged the behavior and sometimes punished them. However, we were grateful when someone told us if one of the children was genuinely disobedient. That's not being a tattletale—it's showing wisdom, discernment, and maturity. I believe reporting to his father showed not that Joseph was a tattletale, but rather that he was a diligent and trustworthy son and worker. Nothing is said to indicate his motives were malicious, and judging by what we know of his character and that of his brothers, he very likely had simply seen or heard something he felt Jacob needed to know.

It takes courage to report evil behavior when the motive is concern for the good of the family, company, or organization, but cowards try to promote themselves through slander or malicious gossip. Whatever Joseph's motives, the Scriptures are clear on matters of the tongue.

What does the apostle Paul say about slander and malicious conversation in Ephesians 4:29–31 and Colossians 3:8?

_____

_____

_____

APPLY   Peer inward for a moment. Do you seek to advance yourself at the expense of others? Do you repeat information (gossip) in a slanderous or malicious manner?

_____

_____

_____

The Coat of Many Colors
Let's take a closer look at Joseph's coat (Genesis 37:3). What could have been so significant about it that his brothers hated him and couldn't even speak a kind word to him? The Hebrew word translated "coat" (k*e*thoneth) can also mean "cover," or "shirt" as a garment or robe. The word for varicolored (pac) means "palm of the hand" or "sole of the foot," by implication a long and sleeved tunic, (divers) colors. These words are used only twice in Scripture—in Genesis they are translated "varicolored tunic" (NASB) and in 2 Samuel "long-sleeved garment." We can't be sure exactly what it looked like but many scholars believe it was a multicolored, long-sleeved garment that reached to the ankles.

Compare Genesis 37:3, 4 with 2 Samuel 13:18.

_____

_____

_____

Who wore the garment in 2 Samuel 13:18?

_____

_____

Sinful actions may cause loss of leadership responsibility.

Based on these verses, why do you think Joseph's coat made his brothers so angry?

_____

_____

Do you see the implication? Joseph's coat was similar to garments worn by the children of kings—a sign of honor, position, and prestige, elevating his status within the family. No wonder the brothers were angry, for apparently Jacob was grooming Joseph to receive the birthright, and he wasn't subtle about his intentions.

Look back to Genesis 29:31, 32. As firstborn in Jacob's family, who would have traditionally received the birthright?

_____

_____

📖 Read Genesis 35:22 and 1 Chronicles 5:1. Why did Reuben lose the birthright?

_____

_____

_____

From memory, try to recall what the birthright entailed.

_____

_____

_____

The son who received the birthright would inherit a double portion of the estate and be head of the family, including spiritually, upon the father's death. Reuben was the eldest son, but when he forfeited his position by sleeping with Bilhah Jacob transferred the firstborn rights to Joseph, his eldest through Rachel. So was Jacob wrong to pick Joseph? Did he choose him based solely on his affection? Remember, neither Isaac nor Jacob was the firstborn son, but God chose them to receive the birthright and blessing. Jacob could have chosen one of his other sons, but none had shown himself worthy of leadership. Simeon and Levi had disgraced the family by leading their brothers in the murderous slaughter at Shechem (Genesis 34), and Dan, Naphtali, Gad, and Asher had exhibited irresponsible behavior in the fields (Genesis 37:2).

Jacob was not so foolish as to turn over control of his family to someone lacking in leadership qualities or spiritual inclination; he had been a wise businessman himself when he worked for Laban, and his own relationship with the Lord had grown immeasurably in the succeeding years. I think Jacob chose Joseph not only from an emotional standpoint, but also from a spiritual and business perspective; he recognized Joseph's leadership potential and his love for the Lord. Subsequent events show that even Joseph's pagan Egyptian masters recognized his exceptional character.

Yet, for Joseph, the coat was a no-win situation. If he didn't wear it he would disappoint his father; if he did wear it his brothers would be reminded he was set apart in regard to affection and position and would despise him all the more. Worst of all, it represented everything they were not—men of moral fiber and integrity. What they didn't understand is that the coat didn't make the man; the man was already made, and the coat was simply the symbol of who Joseph had become.

According to today's text, who exhibited unreasonable favoritism?

_____

_____

The coat was a no-win situation for Joseph. His father wanted him to wear it, and his brothers despised him all the more when they saw it.

Upon whom did the brothers take out their anger?

_____

_____

The brothers were misguided in taking out their anger (and later, revenge) on Joseph. They lashed out at the person who received what they felt entitled to—love, respect, and position. Of course they were hurt and angry, but it was Jacob's preferential treatment that precipitated the problems, not Joseph. The Bible says, *"BE ANGRY, AND YET DO NOT SIN; do not let the sun go down on your anger, and do not give the devil an opportunity"* (Ephesians 4:26, 27). The problem was not that the brothers had negative feelings toward Joseph; the problem is what they did with those feelings. They couldn't change their father's emotions and actions, or their circumstances, but they could have changed their attitudes. Instead of *responding* in a godly manner, they *reacted* in sin. They didn't resolve their anger, and the devil had ample opportunity to wreak havoc in the family.

☐ Read 1 Peter 5:6–8 to see how Joseph's brothers should have responded to their problems.

What should have been their first course of action (v. 6)?

_____

_____

If the brothers had humbled themselves what would God have done for them?

_____

_____

_____

_____

What should have been their second step (v. 7)?

_____

_____

The Greek word translated "casting" (*epirrhipto*) means "to throw upon." The word translated "anxiety" (*merimna*) can also be translated "care, distraction." In other words, we are to throw our cares and distractions on the Lord—not just hand them over, but *throw* them. The idea is to get rid of them and not take them back. Joseph's brothers were certainly burdened with cares and distractions, but they never released them.

APPLY Think of a time you were wrongly displaced in a relationship or when you were passed up for a raise, job, or promotion you deserved. Were you angry? Annoyed? At whom?

_____

_____

_____

_____

When facing a difficult situation, are you a responder or a reactor?

"Casting all your anxiety upon Him, because He cares for you."

I Peter 5:7

Briefly describe the situation and how you handled it.

_____

_____

_____

_____

THE DREAMS: TO TELL OR NOT TO TELL

Pray this verse: *"Open my eyes, that I may behold Wonderful things from Your law."* (Psalm 119:18)

To tell or not to tell—that is the question! Should Joseph have told his dreams to his brothers and father, or should he have kept them to himself? Was he purposely trying to goad them, or was he genuinely concerned about the meaning of his dreams? Respected Bible scholars differ on the answers, but today you're the scholar and can decide for yourself.

I dream virtually every night (and sometimes during my Sunday afternoon nap). Usually I don't recall much of the content, but now and then I remember some details. On occasion I have a nightmare; sometimes I feel as if I'm falling or being chased. Throughout the Scriptures, God spoke to believers and unbelievers in dreams and visions. Unlike our dreams, which we usually recall in fragments, these biblical dreamers could recount theirs in vivid detail. They were confident the dreams held vital significance and, also because the dreams were often disturbing, they were unable to forget them.

There was a long history of God communicating with Joseph's family through dreams and visions. God also actually spoke to, or in the presence of, Abraham, Sarah, Isaac, Rebekah, and Jacob. In this family, whether in dreams, in visions, or face-to-face, when God spoke—people listened; they had confidence His pronouncement would come to pass.

Let's take a look at some familiar dreams and visions in Scripture. After each reference, note who gave the meaning of the dream or vision.

Genesis 20:3–7

Genesis 31:11–13

Genesis 31:24

Genesis 40:8, 9

Genesis 41:15, 16, 28

Daniel 2:1, 19, 28

Daniel 7:13–16

Daniel 8:15–17

Matthew 1:20

Matthew 2:19, 20

Dreams and visions in the Bible were usually of a prophetic nature or carried a warning.

Those who interpreted dreams always relied on God for the explanation and gave Him recognition.

When someone had a dream with divine implications, counsel was sought from others, unless God Himself gave the interpretation or provided one through an angel. Those who did interpret the dreams always relied on God for the explanation and gave Him recognition.

📖 Now read Genesis 37:5–11.

Briefly recount Joseph's dreams.

_____

_____

_____

Who interpreted Joseph's first dream?

_____

_____

What "interpretation" did the brothers give?

_____

_____

_____

What was their response to Joseph?

_____

_____

_____

_____

Who interpreted Joseph's second dream?

_____

_____

What "interpretation" did Jacob give?

_____

_____

_____

What was Jacob's response to Joseph?

_____

_____

Is there any indication Jacob or the brothers sought the Lord before replying to Joseph?

_____

_____

Since dreams and visions were not interpreted by the one who had the dream, it was logical for Joseph to ask his siblings to listen. Some Bible commentators believe he was unwise to share his dreams and others say he was prideful, but these dreams were clearly disturbing enough he felt compelled to seek counsel. Others say it was unnecessary for Joseph to repeat the dreams because the interpretation was clear. But, was it? Is that assumption based on the fact that we now know how the story ends? Pretend for a moment you don't know Joseph becomes vizier of Egypt, then let's look at the verses anew.

"He [Joseph] *said to them, 'Please listen to this dream which I have had'"* (Genesis 37: 6). The King James Version says, *"Hear, I pray you."* Note two important things. First, Joseph was courteous and respectful when speaking to his brothers. Secondly, the Hebrew word translated "hear" (*shama`*) is the same word translated "understand" in Genesis 41:15 (KJV) when Pharaoh asks Joseph to interpret his dreams.

When we read Scripture we don't have the advantage of hearing voice intonations, so it can be difficult to ascertain attitudes or motives, but reconsider Genesis 37:6 when we insert *understand. "And he* [Joseph] *said to them, "Please* [understand] *this dream which I have had."* Although his tone probably wouldn't have mattered since the brothers harbored such deep anger and resentment, it certainly changes the tenor of how one views Joseph's request. He was probably sincerely just asking for an interpretation to his confusing dream, not asserting his position.

Are you beginning to see his dreams in a new light? Hang on, because it gets even more interesting. The words "bowed" (v. 7), "bowing" (v. 9), and "bow" (v. 10) come from the same Hebrew word (*shachah*) meaning "to prostrate oneself," as if to pay homage to royalty or God. The word translated "reign" (*malak*) means "to ascend the throne." The word translated "rule" (*mashal*) means "to reign, govern." All these terms relate to royalty. I always assumed the brothers were jealous and angry because they saw Joseph using his dreams to boast about his future place as head of the household. But that wasn't it at all—at this juncture, his future headship of the family appeared to be a given. They may not have been happy about it, but there was nothing they could do. For Joseph to be chosen to receive the birthright was one thing, but royalty? Ascending to a throne? How could that ever happen?

We need to understand the customs and spiritual mind-set of the Hebrew people. At this point in time they weren't even a nation, just a large family, and they certainly didn't have a king. The only sovereign to whom they bowed and worshipped was Jehovah, their God. For Joseph's dream to insinuate that he would become royalty and his family would bow to him was beyond absurd. This shepherd boy would ascend to a throne? If so, of what country? The boys were well aware the Abrahamic covenant promised they would multiply and become a great nation, but Joseph as king? Ludicrous! The dreams must have seemed outrageous to Joseph as well. No wonder he sought his brothers' counsel in spite of risking their increased anger, even hatred. In his wildest imaginations he wouldn't have dreamed (no pun intended) he would one day end up second only to Pharaoh.

Jacob and his sons could have sought God's counsel but instead hastily reacted by reproaching Joseph with sarcasm and scorn. Even Jacob gave his favorite son a rather harsh reprimand (v. 10), for the Hebrew word translated "rebuked" (*ga`ar*) means "to chide."

Joseph was polite and respectful when sharing his dreams with his family.

Word Study
PAYING HOMAGE

The words translated "bowed," "bowing," and "bow" in Genesis 37 come from the same Hebrew word (*shachah*) meaning "to prostrate oneself" as if to pay homage to royalty or God. "Reign" (*malak*) means "to ascend the throne." "Rule" (*mashal*) means "to reign," "govern." All these terms relate to royalty.

APPLY Have you ever had an idea criticized before you had a chance to fully express it? If so, explain.

_____

_____

_____

_____

How did it make you feel?

_____

_____

_____

Why is it important to listen before you speak?

_____

_____

_____

Do you listen to all the facts *and* the person's heart before you speak?

_____

_____

_____

Would your family consider you to be a *responder* or a *reactor*?

_____

_____

_____

Read Proverbs 18:13. What does the Bible say about a person who speaks out before he hears the entire matter?

_____

_____

_____

_____

Look at Genesis 37:11 again. The reaction of the brothers was one of jealousy. But of what were they jealous? Was it that Joseph was to receive the birthright and had the special coat? Or, was it that he was more loved and exceptionally attractive (Genesis 39:6)? I believe it was all those things and more. The brothers knew the importance of God-given dreams as well as anyone, and now, on top of everything else, Joseph was the recipient of *two* divine dreams. First, favor from their father, and now from God? It must have been almost more than they could bear. But Jacob, who knew from personal experience God-given dreams and visions were to be taken seriously, after his initial reaction, continued to contemplate what he had heard.

I'm sure Joseph spent the next thirteen years while a slave and a prisoner pondering his dreams. Did they give him hope? Were they part of what kept him going? I marvel at Joseph's faith and unwavering obedience when it seemed nothing was going right. In our day, even though we have the complete Scriptures, with all the fulfilled promises Joseph had, many of us find it difficult to trust God.

APPLY Do you find it difficult to trust the Lord to meet your needs and take care of your problems?

_____

_____

_____

What current problem/issue is difficult for you to turn over to Him?

_____

_____

_____

_____

Which promises of God are most helpful when you're going through a difficult trial?

_____

_____

_____

_____

Let's close today's lesson with this encouragement from Psalm 46:1–3, 7, 10a:

_God is our _____ and _____, A very present _____ in _____. Therefore _____ _____ _____ _____, though the earth should _____ And though the mountains _____ into the heart of the sea; Though its waters roar and foam, Though the mountains _____ at its swelling pride. Selah . . . The LORD of hosts is _____ us; The God of Jacob is our _____. Selah . . . _____ _____ and _____ that I am God._

FOR ME TO FOLLOW GOD

Taking Sibling Rivalry to New Heights

DAY FIVE

Pray this verse: _"Open my eyes, that I may behold Wonderful things from Your law."_ (Psalm 119:18)

Congratulations! You've come to the end of the second week of our study on the life of Joseph. I hope you're enjoying these lessons half as much as I enjoyed writing them, and that you're beginning to have new insights as a result of the time you've spent reading and absorbing God's Word.

On Day One we learned the meanings of the names of Jacob's sons and discovered the stormy circumstances surrounding their births. It certainly gives meaning to the phrase *"he lived up to his name,"* for we shall see in our future studies that that is exactly what Joseph's brothers did.

Now, what about you? I hope you did your assignment at the end of Day One.

What is the meaning of your first name?

_____

_____

_____

What is the meaning of your middle name?

_____

_____

_____

Why did your parents choose those names?

_____

_____

Were there any unique circumstances surrounding your birth?

_____

_____

_____

I wish I could read each of your stories because I know they are fascinating. My name is Mary Elizabeth, and I was named for a high school friend of my mother. *Mary* comes from the Hebrew and means "bitter," and *Elizabeth*, also Hebrew, means "consecrated to God" or "God is my oath." I was born into a blended family, and when I was three months old, I was diagnosed with a rare form of cancer and not expected to live. Though my parents didn't know the meaning of my names, they consecrated my life to God at that time. I like that part of my story, but when I found out *Mary* means "bitter," I wasn't so thrilled. However, I determined I didn't have to live up to my name; I don't have to be a bitter person. Instead, I can live the *opposite* of my name, grateful and thankful that when Jesus died on the cross He took the bitterness of my sin upon Himself and gives me the sweetness of eternal life with Him.

Maybe your name had no special significance at the time of your birth other than that your parents simply liked the sound of it. Perhaps you don't like your name because you've been teased or even experienced persecution as a result of a cultural stigma attached to your name, and you'd like to have a new name. I have good news: Jesus has a new identity for you.

When I got married I took my husband's last name because it identified us as one. In a similar manner, when I put my faith in Christ as my Savior, I identified myself with Jesus as a Christian, for I'm *". . . found in Him, not having a righteousness of my own derived from the Law, but that which is through faith in Christ, the righteousness which comes from God on the basis of faith"* (Philippians 3:9). Jesus not only knows and calls us by our names (John 10:1–9; 27–29), but He will give us His name (Revelation 22:3, 4).

After each of the following verses, write out the significance Jesus' name has for our lives.

Matthew 1:21

Matthew 28:19

John 14:13, 14

John 14:26

Acts 4:12

Acts 4:29, 30

1 Corinthians 6:11

Colossians 3:17

1 John 5:13

Word Study
JESUS AND JOSHUA

"Jesus" is the Greek form of the Hebrew name "Joshua," which means "the Lord saves."

The power of Jesus' name is incredible, isn't it? I'll be thrilled and honored to share His name with Him any day! *"Therefore also God highly exalted Him, and bestowed on Him the name which is above every name, that at the name of Jesus EVERY KNEE SHOULD BOW, of those who are in heaven, and on earth, and under the earth, and that every tongue should confess that Jesus Christ is Lord, to the glory of God the Father"* (Philippians 2:9–11 NASB).

As we follow God, we must continue to make wise choices throughout our lives. The first step is to recognize that Jesus is who He says He is, and that He lives up to His name—"the Lord saves." He died on the cross to pay the penalty for our sins, was buried, and rose again. He sacrificed His life in our place so we could have eternal life. Therefore, our first wise choice is to accept Him by faith as our Savior, *the LORD* who saves us.

Following God also means daily making the right choices regardless of circumstances or what our emotions tell us, and that's not always easy. After we've trusted Christ as Savior, and we have the power of the Holy Spirit, doing the right thing is still difficult.

📖 Read Romans 7:14–25 to see how even someone as godly as the apostle Paul struggled.

What happened when Paul wanted to make the right choice (v. 15)?

_____

_____

_____

How could Paul be set free from his battle (vv. 24, 25)?

_____

_____

_____

Others may let you down, but Jesus always lives up to His name!

Making wise choices requires wisdom, and that wisdom must come from the Word of God, our authority. King Solomon, the wise king of Israel, wrote the book of Proverbs

> *for attaining wisdom and discipline; for understanding words of insight; for acquiring a disciplined and prudent life, doing what is right and just and fair; for giving prudence to the simple, knowledge and discretion to the young— let the wise listen and add to their learning, and let the discerning get guidance—for understanding proverbs and parables, the sayings and riddles of the wise. The fear of the LORD is the beginning of knowledge, but fools despise wisdom and discipline.* Proverbs 1:2–7 (NIV)

Don't be discouraged, for learning to make wise decisions based on God's Word takes time and maturity. I know you can do it!

 Heavenly Father, Thank You for giving me a new name, and thank You for loving me enough that You would identify Your name with mine through Your Son Jesus Christ. Thank You, too, for the free gift of eternal life. I pray that You will help me as I try to make wise decisions and choices based on Your Word. Give me the wisdom, understanding, insight, discretion, knowledge, and prudence Solomon speaks of in Proverbs. Help me to fear You and not be a fool who despises wisdom and discipline. Amen.

APPLY Have you consciously put your faith in Jesus, *the LORD who saves*? If not, take a few moments now to acknowledge Him as the one who paid for your sin and gives you the free gift of eternal life. Write out a prayer expressing your thoughts.

_____

_____

_____

_____

_____

_____

_____

_____

_____

_____

_____

_____

Notes

Notes

3

When Life Is the Pits

If we didn't know any better, we might think last week's lesson was describing the behavior of a bunch of preadolescent boys rather than a group of young adults. Instead of acting like mature men, Joseph's brothers fostered resentment and bitterness until their relationship with him was like a pressure cooker ready to explode. And explode it does in this week's lessons.

In the next few days we'll see the extreme measures the brothers took in their dealings with Joseph. In fact, it's almost unbelievable they could treat another human being, let alone their own brother, the way they did. But, if we take a careful personal inventory, we may just recognize some of their attitudes and actions to be similar to our own.

THE POWER OF PEER PRESSURE

Pray this verse: *"Open my eyes, that I may behold Wonderful things from Your law."* (Psalm 119:18)

Have you ever heard the expression, "Show me who your friends are and I'll show you the kind of person you are"? I think it's a true statement, and I feel fortunate most of my close friends have been a positive influence. But even with friends of integrity and good character, I have to admit there were times I caved to pressure and went along with the crowd. Let's be honest—it's hard to stand alone. We all want to be liked; we all want to belong.

📖 Read Genesis 37:12–36.

Sometime before these events took place, Simeon and Levi had launched a murderous mission of revenge on the men of Shechem (Genesis 34). Their sister Dinah had been raped by a young prince, and her brothers sought revenge. Consequently, Jacob and his family moved toward Bethel, and eventually settled in Canaan. So, when his sons headed back to Shechem to pasture the flocks, Jacob was justly concerned for their safety and sent Joseph to discover their well-being. (He eventually found they had moved to fields near Dothan.)

> **"Do not be deceived: 'Bad company corrupts good morals.'"**
>
> **1 Corinthians 15:33**

What started out as a straightforward assignment for Joseph turned into a murderous plot by his brothers, presenting a prime example of the power and dangers of negative peer pressure. Upon seeing his approach, first, one made a spiteful comment, then another responded with a searing jab, and soon the rest joined in the cruel repartee. A few sarcastic remarks turned into a deadly plot.

Shepherds were always on the lookout for danger from wild beasts or robbers, so it was natural Joseph's approach was seen in the distance. They immediately recognized the despised coat that had triggered years of unresolved bitterness and loathing. They began to mock and ridicule Joseph among themselves, feeding off each other's hatred. By the time he reached camp, his murder was planned. They had long since ceased caring if they hurt his feelings, or harmed him physically, for that matter. They must have marveled at their good fortune; the despised brother had shown up out of nowhere with no father to protect him and no witness to their evil deed.

> *Joseph's brothers must have marveled at their good fortune: The despised brother had shown up out of nowhere with no father to protect him and no witness to their evil deed.*

Unchecked emotions can quickly lead to sinful behavior—no wonder the Bible repeatedly warns of the dangers of anger, jealousy, bitterness, and conflict. Anger doesn't always lead to murderous intentions, but if it remains unresolved the inevitable manifestations will be a callous heart and sinful actions.

🛑 **APPLY** Describe a situation in which you followed the crowd and later regretted your conduct.

_____

_____

_____

_____

📖 Read Matthew 18:15–17.

What is Christ's pattern for restoring broken relationships?

_____

_____

_____

How might the relationship between Joseph and his brothers have been different if they had followed a similar pattern?

_____

_____

_____

After each word or phrase, note how the brothers exhibited that particular behavior.

Impulsiveness

_____

_____

Devising evil plans

_____

_____

Failure to take decisive leadership

_____

_____

Lack of conscience

_____

_____

Receiving ill-gotten gain

_____

_____

Disrespecting their father

_____

_____

What potential dangers do you see in unresolved conflict?

As first-born son, Reuben would traditionally have inherited the rights that were now to be bestowed upon Joseph. To Reuben's credit, and though he had the most reason for hating Joseph, he convinced the others to refrain from murder while he secretly planned to rescue Joseph and return him to Jacob. It was an admirable plan, but it failed because Reuben didn't take immediate and decisive leadership. He should have condemned his brothers' actions as sin and protected Joseph from harm, but he didn't have the courage to stand alone and a willingness to take the potential consequences. Hence, when he returned to the pit Joseph was already gone.

Can you imagine Reuben's distress and anguish as *". . . he tore his clothes. He went back to his brothers and said, "The boy isn't there! Where can I turn now?"* (Genesis 37:29–30 NIV). I wonder if it occurred to him he could "turn" and try to catch the Midianite caravan and buy Joseph back. But fear won out, and he went along with the cover-up.

I can picture the other nine men congratulating themselves on their good fortune, justifying their actions, and defending their motives until the magnitude of what they had done finally hit them. Now they had to devise a believable lie to tell their father. It would be twenty-two long years before the brothers would know the fate of Joseph; twenty-two years of guilt, regret, and buried sin; twenty-two years fearing that one of them would break down and tell the truth; twenty-two years of offering insincere condolences and lying to their grieving, brokenhearted father. But worst of all, they were nine men who did not acknowledge, fear, and honor the God of their fathers.

📖 Read Proverbs 28:13.

What does God promise if we hide our sin?

_____

_____

_____

What does God promise if we confess our sin?

_____

_____

📖 Read Proverbs 1:8–19.

Note below the parallels between the wicked companions found in this passage and Joseph's brothers in Genesis.

Wicked Companions	Joseph's Brothers

 Sometimes we need to reevaluate our relationships. Think about which people influence you the most—perhaps relatives, close friends, or business or ministry associates. List them by name in one of the columns:

Godly Influence	Worldly Influence

The Bible is filled with examples of men and women of character and integrity who were willing to stand alone or defend the helpless, forfeiting their lives if necessary—Daniel, Esther, David, Jonathan, the apostle Paul, and more. Chances are we will not be called upon to sacrifice our lives, but we may have to stand in open opposition to a person or group even though it costs us our job, position, or a personal relationship.

Some years ago, my husband, Bill, took a stand for truth and integrity knowing it might cost him his job—our only source of income. The children and I stood behind his decision though there were anxious days while we faced the unknown. Fortunately he retained his position, but we had been willing to make the sacrifice.

When our son David was in middle school, his soccer team was playing in the finals for a gold medal—not the World Cup, but exciting, nonetheless. A teammate's mother misunderstood the game time and arrived with her son at halftime. As they approached the stands, one of the fathers rose to his feet and verbally berated the poor woman—she was irresponsible, a bad mother, she'd let down the team, and so on. Everyone turned, mouths agape. I looked around waiting for someone to defend the poor woman now in tears. No one moved. He continued his tirade; still no one moved. I couldn't hold back. I worked my way to the far end of the bleachers, and stood between the defenseless mother and the irate man. I don't recall my exact words, but—I let him have it! He was so shocked that anyone would stand up to him (he'd been loud and obnoxious all season) he backed into his seat and kept silent for the remainder of the game. Later, the mother and several other parents expressed their gratitude.

We no longer see those people, but believe me, our children will never forget that their parents stood for truth and defended the helpless.

 Describe a time when you had to stand alone for truth or defend the helpless.

_____

_____

_____

Today's study has been difficult to write because I've had times in the past when I've tried to justify my wrong behavior, and I haven't always had the courage to stand alone. Perhaps it has stirred some troubled memories for you, too. I think we've all been guilty of succumbing to peer pressure, though hopefully not to the degree of Joseph's brothers. Before you protest, think of that time on the playground when you joined the other children in cruel name-calling. Perhaps there was a time in junior or senior high school you didn't defend the girl who wasn't invited to the party, yet you knew her heart was broken.

Those actions could be attributed to youthful immaturity, but what about today? Do you yield to peer pressure by speaking or listening to gossip, sloughing off with other employees, or cheating on your income tax because "everyone else does it"? What about when you know a decision or situation is not biblical and may hurt the integrity of a business, organization, or church? Do you stand for truth against the crowd, or do you look the other way?

_____

_____

_____

_____

_____

_____

Let's close today with a message from Psalm 15:

> LORD, *who may dwell in your sanctuary? Who may live on your holy hill? He whose walk is blameless and who does what is righteous, who speaks the truth from his heart and has no slander on his tongue, who does his neighbor no wrong and casts no slur on his fellowman, who despises a vile man but honors those who fear the* LORD, *who keeps his oath even when it hurts, . . . He who does these things will never be shaken.* (vv. 1–5 NIV)

When Life Is the Pits

DAY TWO

THE PIT: MY BROTHERS THREW ME WHERE?

Pray this verse: *"Open my eyes, that I may behold Wonderful things from Your law."* (Psalm 119:18)

I s there someone you know whose very presence makes your life miserable? I'm not just talking about someone who's a nuisance, but someone you'd like to have *out of your life*—I mean *gone*! Perhaps you've had thoughts like, *If only they would move, or find another job, or go to another church, or* . . . Maybe you've gone so far as to think, *If that person was dead, life would be so much easier.*

No doubt, Joseph's brothers entertained such fantasies about him. It wasn't just that he was their father's favorite, was exceptionally good-looking, would receive the birthright, wore that incredible coat, and that his mother had been the beloved wife while their own mothers were treated as second-rate. Yes, it was all that, but what they really must have dreaded was that those dreams might be fulfilled. And yet, "The presence of Joseph in the home didn't *create* problems so much as *reveal* them."[1]

56   FOLLOWING GOD – JOSEPH: BEYOND THE COAT OF MANY COLORS

📖 Review Genesis 37:18–28 to get a complete picture of this wicked plot.

What was the brothers' original plan for Joseph (vv. 19, 20)?

_____

_____

_____

What was Reuben's plan (vv. 21, 22)?

_____

_____

_____

What did the brothers finally do to Joseph?

_____

_____

I find it amazing that nine of Jacob's sons had no qualms about murdering their younger brother. If not for Reuben's intervention, Joseph would have been dead within minutes of arriving at the camp. Ultimately, they agreed to let Joseph die a "natural" death in the pit instead of doing the deed themselves, yet their objective was the same. Imagine Joseph's shock and confusion when his brothers began taunting and pushing him, tearing off his coat, and finally forcing him into the cistern. He knew they despised him, but this was taking their hatred to new depths—literally. Stripping him of his coat was a particularly spiteful attempt at humiliation. The garment represented everything about him the brothers hated—their father's affection and favoritism, the birthright, but worst of all, Joseph's future authority over them. To symbolically strip him of his future position of family leadership must have seemed a great triumph.

But even though they took away his coat, threw him in a pit, and sold him as a slave, they couldn't take away God's calling for Joseph's life. To the contrary, without knowing it, they were playing right into God's hand.

The pit into which Joseph was thrown was likely a dry water cistern. Rainfall was scarce in the area, and cisterns were needed to store water for drinking and irrigation. Though the size and form varied, some were shaped like a bell or a bottle with the narrow end at the top making escape virtually impossible. Whatever the size and shape of Joseph's pit, we can only imagine the fear and anguish he must have endured. What was inside? Snakes? Insects? Was it dark? Cold? Did Joseph suffer from claustrophobia? Although it appears his time in the pit was brief, I'm sure it seemed like forever to him.

What did the brothers do after they threw Joseph in the pit (v. 25)?

_____

_____

_____

_____

No one can take away God's calling for your life.

✏️ *Did You Know?*
? **DRY CISTERNS**

Dry cisterns were occasionally used as prisons (Jeremiah 38:6), and archaeologists have even found evidence of cisterns being used to dispose of or bury bodies

(http://www.bible-history.com/biblestudy/cisterns.html).

What was Joseph doing while his brothers plotted against him (Genesis 42:21)?

_____

_____

_____

Imagine the extreme callousness of the brothers as they sat down to eat while their brother languished in terror, begging for his life in the dark recesses. Picture them laughing and jesting, maybe wagering on how long it would take for him to die.

What was the brothers' final solution (Genesis 37:25–27)?

_____

_____

_____

Problem solved! The brothers would "show mercy" by not killing Joseph, and sell him to slave traders instead. With minimal guilt, they would be rid of the despised brother. But, as we'll see in the coming weeks, their actions solved nothing and simply led to more sin. Without anticipating the consequences, the boys had created, and were trapped in, a pit of their own.

Describe a time when you knowingly made a sinful choice that spiraled into further wrong choices.

_____

_____

_____

_____

Your pit may have been forced upon you by others, or be one of your own making. Either way, God wants to deliver you. He may not do it immediately, and the way He does it may not be to your liking, but God is faithful.

You and I will probably never be held captive or thrown into a literal cistern, but occasionally we will find ourselves in other kinds of pits. These "pits" may be of our own making, or generated by the words or actions of another. When someone says, "I'm in the pits," they're usually talking about being emotionally disheartened, or even clinically depressed. Emotional pits can cause nearly as much anguish as Joseph must have felt in his literal pit—fear and hopelessness with no way out.

APPLY If you are presently in a "pit," describe the circumstances (or describe a past pit experience). If not, praise the Lord!

_____

_____

_____

_____

Describe your emotions during the experience.

_____

_____

_____

📖 Read Psalm 40 to see how King David dealt with his pit. How do these verses give you hope?

_____

_____

_____

What was David's attitude as he waited for the Lord (v. 1)?

_____

_____

_____

What did God do for David (vv. 2, 3)?

_____

_____

_____

Joseph was surely relieved when his brothers lifted him from the pit, but I doubt he felt as if his feet were on solid rock on his journey to Egypt—and yet they were. Joseph was exactly where he was supposed to be. Like Joseph, your "pit" may not be resolved exactly the way you've hoped or planned, but you can be confident you are in God's care. You can say with David, *"I delight to do Your will, O my God; Your Law is within my heart"* (v. 8).

I can't help but wonder if Jacob, Rachel, and Leah ever made a conscious effort to build strong relationships between their children. When they heard the kids quarrel, did they take time to moderate the dispute? Did Jacob really _listen_ to the frustrations of his sons? Did he even try to conceal his favoritism for Joseph? Why didn't he deal decisively with Reuben when the young man slept with Bilhah, or with Simeon and Levi when they murdered the men in Shechem?

The solution seems so simple, but then I consider myself. How many times have my own children seen my husband and me angry with each other, purse our lips, and walk away instead of solving the problem as mature adults? Too many times, I'm afraid. I recall times when my children argued with each other and I forced them to apologize. Too often, they apologized through clenched teeth, all the while seething inside. To my shame, I didn't always take the time to listen; to show how they had hurt their brother or sister; to explain why their sin displeased the Lord and the importance of forgiveness. It was easier not to deal with the problem, but it solved nothing.

And then, I think of the pit. Sure the brothers were upset with Joseph, but they could have given him a quick update on the flocks and sent him back to dad. No pit, no plot, no pain. That's what they _should have_ done.

It's easy to judge and criticize them, for they were so blatantly evil—I'd like to throw _them_ into a pit myself! But, while writing today's lesson, I've been convicted of the times when, by my sharp words or inconsiderate actions, I've thrown someone else into a pit of frustration or despair. How often did I listen to my children's chatter halfheartedly, or decline to play a game because I was "too busy," or shoot down an idea because I thought mine was

> **"Do not withhold your mercy from me, O LORD; may your love and your truth always protect me. For troubles without number surround me; my sins have overtaken me, and I cannot see. They are more than the hairs of my head, and my heart fails within me. Be pleased, O LORD, to save me; O LORD, come quickly to help me."**
>
> **Psalm 40:11–13 (NIV)**

better? How many times have I "sat down to eat" when I knew someone was hurting and ignored their silent pleas for help? And worst of all, how many times have I figuratively pulled a person out of the pit, giving them hope, only to sell them into slavery by rejection, by not following through with a promise, or by some other means?

What are some other ways we throw people into emotional pits?

_____

_____

_____

_____

APPLY Prayerfully consider. Are there any people you've put into a pit to whom you need to make amends?

_____

_____

_____

Fellow believers, let's strive to lift people *out of* the pit rather than push people *into* the pit.

Note: Are you, or is someone you know, in a pit of despair and hopelessness? Are you on the verge of divorce, having thoughts of suicide, abusing drugs or alcohol, or dealing with other serious issues? Whether the pit is of your own making or, like Joseph's, forced upon you by others, please realize that it is extremely important to seek help from a counselor or other qualified person.

When Life Is the Pits

TWENTY PIECES OF SILVER: IS THAT ALL I'M WORTH?

Pray this verse: *"Open my eyes, that I may behold Wonderful things from Your law."* (Psalm 119:18)

📖 Please read Genesis 37:25–36.

Who was the mastermind behind the scheme to sell Joseph?

_____

_____

_____

Did any of the brothers appear to object to the plan?

_____

_____

_____

According to Acts 7:9, what was the motivation for selling their brother?

_____

_____

_____

Can you recall another member of the family who profited financially in the midst of sin (Genesis 12:10–16)?

_____

_____

_____

The Hebrew word translated "profit" (betsa`) means "plunder, gain."

Judah, the fourth son of Leah, assumed leadership when Reuben left camp. When he saw the caravan, he began formulating a new plan: Forget leaving Joseph in the cistern to die—why not make a little profit and avoid the guilt of murder?

Close your eyes for a moment and picture the scene in your mind. Can you hear Joseph begging for his life, pleading to be taken back to his father, promising not to reveal what they had done? Can you sense his panic as his brothers negotiate with the Midianites? Do you feel his anguish as he tries to persuade the merchants to cancel the transaction, reminding them that they are, in fact, distant cousins, for they are all descended from Abraham?

How quickly the events of these few verses transpired! Joseph begged, but no one listened; no one cared about a scared seventeen-year-old shepherd boy whose life would never be the same. Instead, a price of twenty pieces of silver was agreed upon, and Joseph was on his way to Egypt. In a matter of hours, Joseph had gone from dreaming to dreading; from favored son to frantic slave.

If the brothers had misgivings about what they had done, they no doubt relieved their guilty feelings by reminding themselves Joseph was finally out of their lives forever. After all, of what were they really guilty? They hadn't murdered him; they were just resolving a few family issues. Joseph was headed to a country that despised Hebrews, so he would never receive the birthright, he would never rule over them, and he would never ascend to a position of royalty. His fate was sealed, and their problems were over. They could resume life as it had been before that wretched boy was born. And, as an added measure of satisfaction, each brother had received two silver coins in the exchange!

True Value
Two pieces of silver for each man—twenty pieces of silver total. That was the value placed on Joseph's life—his future, his fears, his feelings. His brothers had committed him into the hands of total strangers and a life of adversity and servitude, because they didn't value him as a person.

What do you think the brothers valued?

_____

_____

_____

Did You Know?
ISHMAELITE

The term "Ishmaelite" was sometimes used to refer to several interrelated tribal groups. The Ishmaelites and Midianites were both descended from Abraham.

The Midianites traded various items including oils, scents, balms, and foodstuffs, but they were also well-known slave traders.

Your value is not based on what others think of you, rather what God thinks of you.

What do you think Joseph valued?

_____

_____

_____

Joseph's brothers wanted what he had, you might even say they *valued* what he had—respect, position, leadership, their father's affection, but they didn't want to live a life of obedience and integrity; they didn't *value* the process through which one attains those goals. And if they couldn't have them, they didn't want Joseph to have them.

Joseph, on the other hand, valued faithfulness, obedience, and godly character. He understood that the *process* of living a godly life is what brings glory to God and, in the end, that that's all that matters. Joseph could have elected to go along with his brothers from an early age; he could have chosen to approve of, and even join his brothers in, their wicked behavior in Shechem and their poor work ethic (or ethics) in the fields. He could have chosen to endorse Reuben's immorality with Bilhah. But Joseph's values weren't manmade, and instead he chose to live by God's value system and please Him.

According to Galatians 1:10, whom are we to please?

_____

_____

For much of my life I was, and every now and then still am, a people-pleaser. That's another way of saying I sometimes place too much value on what others think about me. Perhaps it has something to do with my upbringing; perhaps I just want to feel accepted. But do you know what? I'm not going to blame my faults on the past; I'm not going to wallow in *should haves* and *shouldn't haves*. No, I'm going to strive to please my Savior instead.

In the first column list some things you think the world values. In the second column list what you think God values.

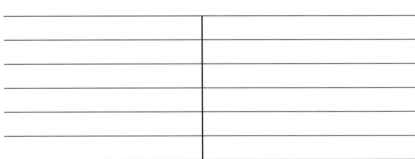

The World Values:	God Values:

 Now look back. In the first column circle each item in which you think you place *too* much value. In the second column circle those things in which you need to place *more* value. Man's values change, tending to adapt to the culture, but God's value system never changes. That's why it's so important for us to establish our beliefs and principles on the Word of God (Hebrews 13:8) rather than man's philosophies, circumstances, or emotions.

A certain hair color company once used the slogan "Because I'm worth it" in answer to why someone would spend more money for their product. The advertisements were brilliant. They appealed to the egos of consumers who were willing to pay a little more because they felt they were worth the extra price.

In God's economy we are worth it. After each verse below, note how God shows us our worth to Him.

Genesis 1:27

_____

_____

Psalm 121

_____

_____

Psalm 139:1–5

_____

_____

Matthew 6:25, 26

_____

_____

1 Peter 1:18, 19

_____

_____

Several years ago my mother-in-law gave me a Wedgwood tea set I had often admired in her china cabinet. She knew I loved Wedgwood, so her gift was especially meaningful to me. Because the set was old and unusual, I knew it would be expensive to replace, so I took special care of it. But I didn't know its real worth until I saw an identical set in an antiques store priced at $850! The antiques dealer was an expert and priced it accordingly. When I understood the true value of my tea set, my appreciation for it increased.

We need to know and appreciate our value because the Expert knows our worth. You and I are worth the very life of God's Son, the Lord Jesus Christ. Why did He die for you and me? *Because we're worth it!*

It's All in Your Perspective
For the last two years I've been reassessing the value I put on possessions. I've been purging my house—not emptying it, but getting rid of excess "stuff." (Not my Wedgwood tea set, though!) If my kids don't want it, I'm selling it in a garage sale or giving it away. It's not that I don't like pretty things, or that I think it's wrong to own them, but they just don't have the same importance they once had. I find I'm satisfied to enjoy the memories of my "stuff," and I don't need to hang on to it. Perhaps it's because, as I'm getting older, I'm learning to have a different perspective and to value what will make a difference for eternity: time invested in others, money spent on

> **"Knowing that you were not redeemed with perishable things like silver or gold from your futile way of life inherited from your forefathers, but with precious blood, as of a lamb unblemished and spotless, the blood of Christ."**
>
> **1 Peter 1:18, 19**

needs more than wants, talents and gifts used wisely. When I make decisions and choices, I've begun to ask myself, *In light of eternity, will this matter?* I'm learning to live with an eternal perspective; I'm learning to have "God values."

APPLY How might your eternal perspective need to change?

_____

_____

_____

_____

WHEN YOUR LIFE IS OUT OF CONTROL

Pray this verse: *"Open my eyes, that I may behold Wonderful things from Your law."* (Psalm 119:18)

📖 Read Genesis 37:25, 36.

The caravan route to Egypt was more than two hundred tortuous miles. Providing for trade stops along the way, the journey would likely have taken between two and three weeks. Travel conditions were dangerous and difficult for the traders, but even more so for the slaves.

Although we can't know exactly what Joseph was thinking and feeling at this point, I think it's safe to say he felt as if his life was out of control. His father had given him the simple task of checking on the welfare of his brothers, and he obeyed even though he knew they hated him. He acted in obedience, he did the right thing. How could this possibly be happening to him? Okay, the pit was bad enough, but now, slavery? Egypt? His dreams had turned into a nightmare.

The Lord had not abandoned Joseph, though to the human mind it would seem all hope was lost. On the contrary, God used slave traders to deliver him from the hands of his murderous brothers. The very people who bought Joseph to turn a profit by selling him into a life of slavery were the ones God used to bring Joseph to the center of His plans.

Because you know how the story ends, and you can see the complete picture, describe how you think God was directing Joseph's caravan.

_____

_____

_____

I love this next part, and I think you will, too. The Hebrew word translated "caravan" in Genesis 37:25 is *'or^echah* and means just that—"a traveling company." Now read Psalm 27:11 and Proverbs 3:5, 6. The word translated "path(s)" in these passages is the Hebrew word *'orach* and can also be translated as a "well-trodden road" or "caravan route." An *'or^echah* (a traveling company or caravan) would have traveled on an *'orach* (path, well-trodden road). Do you see the implication? God was leading Joseph's caravan on a well-trodden road. God knew exactly where Joseph was going. *"Trust in the LORD with all your heart, And lean not on your own understanding; In all your ways acknowledge Him, And He shall direct your paths* [caravans]" (Proverbs 3:5, 6 NKJV).

It's obvious to us God was in control and directing Joseph's caravan to Egypt, because *we know the end of Joseph's story.* I've mentioned this before, and I will several more times throughout the course of our study—remember; don't forget; tie a string around your finger! *God knows the end of your story, too*—He is directing *your 'or^echah* (caravan) on *your 'orach* (path)!

How does it make you feel to know that God is directing your caravan?

_____

_____

_____

📖 Read Isaiah 55:8, 9 and Jeremiah 29:11.

How do these verses help give you comfort and understanding when you are facing difficult circumstances?

_____

_____

_____

APPLY   Describe a time when you thought your circumstances were completely out of your control, but later you were able to see how the Lord had been directing your caravan.

_____

_____

_____

_____

After walking on rugged terrain in shackles for hundreds of miles, Joseph's body probably had more than superficial bruising. The restraints rubbing against his skin could have produced oozing sores that possibly left lifelong scars. But perhaps most difficult of all was the endless time Joseph had for thinking—trudging mile after mile with no end in sight; the sleepless nights, tossing and turning, trying to find a comfortable position in which to sleep, struggling to keep warm in the frigid desert.

Try to imagine some of the things Joseph may have been thinking and feeling and write them below.

_____

_____

_____

Remember; don't forget; tie a string around your finger! God knows the end of your story, too—He is directing your 'orechah (caravan) on your 'orach (path)!

> **I can picture Joseph glancing back at the horizon every so often and thinking, Surely, my brothers will realize their wrong; surely, they will change their minds and come after me.**

At the top of my own list is *fear*—fear of the unknown, fear of abandonment, fear of the future—fear there might not even *be* a future. I can picture Joseph glancing back at the horizon every so often and thinking, *Surely, my brothers will realize their wrong; surely, they will change their minds and come after me.*

Too often I find myself in a state of fear instead of trust. Two Scripture verses are particularly comforting to me during those times. I've committed them to memory, and when I begin to give way to my fears, I recite these verses.

"When I am afraid, I will put my trust in You" (Psalm 56:3). It's short and gets right to the point. The Hebrew word translated "trust" (*batach*) means to have "confidence" or a "place of refuge, safety." What is more comforting than to know that the Lord is our refuge? We can never be confident in our circumstances no matter how much we try to be in control, for circumstances are always changing. Yet God never changes, and we can always be secure in Him.

The second verse says, *"For God has not given us a spirit of fear, but of power and of love and of a sound mind"* (2 Timothy 1:7 NKJV). Since fear doesn't come from God, we know it comes from our enemy Satan. I don't know about you, but I would rather have the power, love, and a sound mind that are confidently found in the Lord than the fear that can eat away at the mind and body.

📖 Read Philippians 4:6–8. When we prayerfully take our worries and concerns to the Lord with thanksgiving, what will He use to guard our hearts and minds?

_____

_____

_____

What eight things are we told to think about in verse 8?

_____

_____

_____

_____

> **We can never be confident in our circumstances no matter how much we try to be in control, because circumstances are always changing. Yet, God never changes, and we can always be secure in Him.**

Some might say it's impossible to control what we think and how we feel, but the Scriptures say otherwise. The Greek word translated "guard" (*phroureo*) in verse 7 is a military term that means "to be a watcher in advance" as if a sentinel, or "to hem in, protect." I may not be able to stop a thought from passing through my mind, but I can stop it from taking control of my mind. The word translated "hearts" is a Greek word (*kardia*) that includes our thoughts and feelings. God will place His peace as a sentinel or guard over our "thoughts" and "feelings." By controlling what we think, we *can* control our actions.

Although the Bible says nothing negative about Joseph, it's important to remember he was human just as we are; he, too, experienced fears and doubts. I believe the way he dealt with those fears and doubts is what got him through that journey to Egypt and the subsequent years of testing and turmoil—he allowed God's peace to guard his thoughts and emotions.

APPLY Describe a time when prayer and Scripture helped you overcome your fears.

_____

_____

_____

_____

The journey to Egypt would have been a good time for Joseph to pull out his handy pocket-size Bible and get some encouragement from the book of Psalms, or from the lives of other Bible greats who had walked through difficult trials. But he didn't have the Scriptures as we do today; he only had the testimonies passed down through his forefathers. I believe those reminders of God's faithfulness and promises to Abraham, Isaac, and Jacob helped Joseph through the long days and nights. We are so much more fortunate than Joseph! We have the promises of God through the completed Scriptures for our encouragement and direction (2 Timothy 3:16, 17), as well as the testimonies of those who have gone before us.

Most people base their outlook on their circumstances. If things are running smoothly they are happy and God is good, but if circumstances are not what they expected or desired, God has deserted them and life stinks. Their emotions run parallel to their circumstances.

If your life seems beyond your control, cheer up—you are probably exactly where God wants you! Think about what a great place that is to be—so out of control there is absolutely nothing for you to do but go to the Lord for refuge! That is when God can really begin to work in your life: when all human hope is gone; when there is nothing left but Him. Joseph's caravan trip to Egypt was such a time for him. He was a godly young man, but for him as for all of us, there came a time when he needed to be broken and to experience a death to his dreams. Up until this time, his direction seemed sure: He was being groomed to become head of the household; he had wealth and security; he was the favored son of a prosperous herder; he knew where his "caravan" was headed.

You, too, may have thought the direction of your life was laid out in a nice, clear, smooth path, but now you've been sold into slavery. Stop right there! Go to the Lord for refuge; give Him control of your circumstances; let him direct your caravan. God can fulfill His purposes for your life in ways you can never imagine. He _". . . is able to do exceeding abundantly beyond all that we ask or think, according to the power that works within us"_ (Ephesians 3:20).

Remember that God knows the end of your story from the very beginning, and if there was ever a story to remind us of that truth, it is Joseph's. Though all seemed lost, God was watching over him each step of the way. He is watching over you, too!

If your life seems beyond your control, cheer up—you are probably exactly where God wants you!

FOR ME TO FOLLOW GOD

Pray this verse: *"Open my eyes, that I may behold Wonderful things from Your law."* (Psalm 119:18)

If the importance of following God was ever clearly seen, it has been in each of our lessons this week.

On the first day I challenged you to take inventory of your attitudes and actions as we watched the drama continue to unfold. Did you see yourself in any of our lessons?

At this point in our narrative, it would appear Joseph's brothers were getting away with murder—well, perhaps not murder, but kidnapping and slave trading, anyway. They had finally gotten rid of that goody-two-shoes Joseph; no one knew what they had done (except themselves and a few Midianites on their way to Egypt), and none of them would dare tell anyone else. Now perhaps they would get the affection they always wanted from their father, and one of *them* would receive the birthright. Joseph's ridiculous dreams would never come to pass, and they wouldn't have to worry about him reporting back to Dad on their work ethic or moral behavior. The cash in their pockets wasn't so bad, either. Yes, life was good for these ten sons of Jacob!

It's been said, "Crime doesn't pay," but sadly, there are times when, in the short term, some people do profit from wrongdoing. It can be frustrating when you try to be obedient to the Lord and everything goes right for the bad guy and nothing seems to go right for you. I'm pretty sure Joseph had similar thoughts about his brothers on his journey to Egypt. The more he tried to do right, the more things seemed to go wrong.

📖 Let's read Psalm 37:1–10 to help us gain some understanding into this sometimes frustrating dilemma.

What shouldn't we do when we see someone doing wrong (v. 1)?

_____

_____

What will eventually happen to those who do evil?

_____

_____

_____

_____

List everything we should do when those around us are doing evil.

_____

_____

_____

I'll admit there are times I've fretted over these very issues, but then I remember that no one gets away with anything! *"Nothing in all creation is hidden from God's sight. Everything is uncovered and laid bare before the eyes of him to whom we must give account"* (Hebrews 4:13 NIV).

This week you have read and reread parts of Genesis 37 several times. By now, you should be able to recall the events fairly well. Think back over the text. Did it occur to you there were any number of pivotal points in Joseph's story when the outcome could have been completely turned around with just one wise choice? If any of his brothers had taken a stand against the others, gone to his father, and tried to make things right, it would have been so different. But they continued to make poor choices and act out according to their pent-up hatred. Reuben, at least, attempted to do the right thing, but even he didn't carry through after his initial plan went awry. In the end, they all went along with the crowd.

Read the following questions and rate yourself on a scale of 1 to 10 (10 being a definite *yes* and 1 being a definite *no*).

Do you consistently stand for truth and integrity even if it means you must stand alone?

1   2   3   4   5   6   7   8   9   10

Are you easily swayed by the opinions of others?

1   2   3   4   5   6   7   8   9   10

Do you speak out when you hear gossip or disparaging remarks about another person?

1   2   3   4   5   6   7   8   9   10

How would others rate you on your willingness to stand against negative peer pressure?

1   2   3   4   5   6   7   8   9   10

Getting through the challenges of the teenage years has always been hard, but standing up to peer pressure in that stage of life is particularly difficult. One of the things I love about Joseph's story is the details given about that time of his life. Remember, he was only seventeen years old, but he was already being groomed to be the spiritual head and leader of his family, God's chosen people. It's true that children grew up faster and were given more responsibility in the ancient Hebrew culture, but young Joseph demonstrated more maturity, integrity, and godly character than any of his ten older brothers. In addition to that, God had given him two dreams with significant implications. Joseph was a young man who stood up to peer pressure from his brothers throughout his life.

The Progression of Sin

Have you ever noticed that sin is progressive? It starts with a thought and evolves into action. Gossip is a thought that shouldn't be shared. Adultery starts as an innocent relationship that leads to lustful thoughts, a flirtatious remark, and finally, an immoral act. Thieves begin by thinking about and desiring something they don't have, and eventually they steal it. Murder begins with angry thoughts, then unresolved conflict, and ultimately, deadly results. You get the picture—if the thoughts and emotions are not dealt

"Nothing in all creation is hidden from God's sight. Everything is uncovered and laid bare before the eyes of him to whom we must give account."

Hebrews 4:13 (NIV)

with, they begin a progression into sin. The thought becomes desire, and desire becomes action.

Joseph's brothers didn't rein in their thoughts and emotions, and the sequence began. It's hard to imagine they could have gone from mocking to murder in the short time it took Joseph to approach their camp, but it happened because they had started the progression of sin years before in their thought process.

Carefully read the following verse: *"Let the words of my mouth and the meditation of my heart Be acceptable in Thy sight, O LORD, my rock and my Redeemer"* (Psalm 19:14). After looking up several words from this verse in my concordance, I've turned those words into a prayer that is meaningful to me. "Lord, may every word that comes out of my mouth, and every feeling, every desire, and every thought I have, give you pleasure and delight." How different our lives would be if we *prayed* that prayer everyday; if we *lived* that prayer every moment.

Ask yourself the following questions:

Do my words delight the Lord?

_____
_____
_____
_____

Do my desires give God pleasure?

_____
_____
_____
_____

Do my feelings and emotions please Him?

_____
_____
_____

Are my thoughts a delight to the Lord?

_____
_____
_____

According to Philippians 2:1–5, we should have an attitude like Christ's. We should think as He thinks; and if we think as He thinks, we will be more inclined to act as He acts.

How should Joseph's brothers have exemplified an attitude like Christ's when:

> **Lord, may every word that comes out of my mouth, and every feeling, every desire, and every thought I have, give you pleasure and delight.**

Joseph brought his father a bad report about their work in the field?

_____

_____

Jacob gave Joseph the special coat?

_____

_____

Jacob showed greater love for Joseph in other ways?

_____

_____

Joseph shared his dreams?

_____

_____

Joseph went to the fields near Dothan to check on them?

_____

_____

Judah suggested selling Joseph to the Midianites?

_____

_____

The brothers returned home to Jacob?

_____

_____

 Heavenly Father, I know my actions are not always pleasing to you, because my thoughts are not always pleasing to you. I know I've failed you many times, and I ask you to forgive me. I want to think more like Christ; I want to act more like Christ; I want to delight You and give You pleasure. In order to do that, I know I must spend more time with You in prayer and meditating on Your Word. Father, more times than I'd like to admit, I've had attitudes similar to those of Joseph's brothers. I also know there are times when I've been a "pit pusher"; help me now to become a "pit lifter." In Jesus' name, amen.

Works Cited

1. Warren W. Wiersbe, *Be Authentic* (Colorado Springs: Victor Cook Communications Ministries, 1997), 78.

Notes

4

I Didn't Apply for This Job

Was there ever a time when you were a child that you felt like running away from home? Maybe you felt as if you weren't being treated fairly, or you were angry with your parents or siblings. Perhaps there are days even now when you feel like running away! When finances, relationships, or other situations go awry, and nothing you try seems to work, the natural tendency is to want to get away from the problem.

This week we'll see how Judah wanted to run *away* from home (and did), and we'll also see how Joseph wanted to run *to* home (but couldn't). Joseph didn't want to learn a new language; he didn't want to dress in the clothes of a different culture; he didn't want to work in some stranger's house. He didn't apply for this job!

Joseph's life was out of control—or was it? Life hadn't prepared him to be a slave in a foreign country—or had it?

NO PLACE TO HIDE: YOU CAN'T RUN FROM GOD

Pray this verse: *"Open my eyes, that I may behold Wonderful things from Your law."* (Psalm 119:18)

Welcome to Week Four. Today we'll study events that set the stage for our remaining weeks. So, pay close attention and bear with me, and by the end of Week Eight it will all come together. Let's get right to it.

📖 Begin by reading Genesis 37:31–36 and all of Genesis 38.

The jump from Joseph (Genesis 37) to Judah (Genesis 38) may, at first reading, seem like an odd break in our lessons, but as 2 Timothy 3:16 says, *"All Scripture is inspired by God and profitable for teaching, for reproof, for correction, for training in righteousness."* We'll come right back to Judah and Tamar, but first let's back up a few verses.

Did you notice that only two of the ten brothers are mentioned by name in Genesis 37? Can you recall which two? Write their names below. Here's a hint: One wanted to rescue Joseph (v. 21) and the other masterminded the plan to sell him to the Midianites (v. 26).

_____

_____

> **"All Scripture is inspired by God and profitable for teaching, for reproof, for correction, for training in righteousness."**
>
> **2 Timothy 3:16**

Reuben wanted to save Joseph and return him to their father, and Judah came up with the idea of selling him into slavery. Remember those two names, because they play key roles in Joseph's story.

Describe the brothers' plan for hiding their sin from their father (Genesis 37:31, 32).

_____

_____

_____

Years earlier, Jacob had been involved in a similar scheme to deceive. Read Genesis 27:6–17. What similarities do you see between the two events?

_____

_____

_____

> **After more than thirty years, Jacob was still reaping what he had sowed.**
>
> **(Galatians 6:7)**

All of us learn by example, and children in particular tend to mirror the behavior to which they are exposed. Though Joseph and his brothers saw *some* examples of faith and obedience in their forefathers, Jacob, Rachel, and Leah raised them in an environment of jealousy and deceit, passiveness to sin, and sometimes even indifference to God's direction. I wonder if they really expected their children to react differently than they did when faced with similar circumstances.

Answer the following questions based on what we've learned so far.

What did Joseph and his brothers learn about:

• Getting along with siblings, from Jacob and Esau?

_____

_____

_____

• Love and respect for siblings, from Rachel and Leah?

_____

_____

_____

• Keeping your word, from Grandpa Laban?

_____

_____

_____

• The Lord's plan for a godly marriage, from Jacob, Rachel, and Leah?

_____

_____

_____

• Patiently waiting to receive the promises of God, from Abraham, Isaac, and Jacob?

_____

_____

_____

The brothers reacted to conflict just as their parents and grandparents had. Want the birthright? Take it by deceit. Got conflict with your brother? Leave home. Don't like your wife? Take two—or four! Want a baby right now? Sleep with the maid. Got problems? Don't worry—think of a plan—any plan; if it sounds good and feels right, just do it!

So when the time arrived—Brother Joseph annoys you? Want him out of the way? No problem; sell him to slave traders and pocket the change. Like father, mothers, and grandparents—like sons!

According to Genesis 37:33, what conclusion did Jacob arrive at when he saw Joseph's bloody coat?

_____

_____

The brothers thought getting rid of Joseph would solve their problems, but alas, it only created new ones.

People did not grieve quietly in the Hebrew culture. They wept and wailed, tore their clothing, and covered their heads with ashes.

Even without seeing a body, Jacob immediately assumed Joseph was dead. But think back to the dreams. Though Jacob rebuked Joseph, he did give credence to them. The inference of the dreams had been that Joseph had a great future. If Jacob had paid more heed to their implications his grief may have been lessened and his faith increased. Perhaps he would have had hope that God had a plan and his eleventh son might still be alive. But Jacob was convinced of Joseph's death and would not be comforted; no matter what his children said or did, he was inconsolable. And people did not grieve silently in that culture. They wept and wailed, moaned and groaned. Everyone in the encampment would have been keenly aware of Jacob's intense misery.

What do you think the atmosphere in Jacob's home was like during this time?

_____

_____

_____

No doubt, Joseph became even larger in death than he had been in life. Have you ever noticed how people are romanticized in death? Their faults are diminished, and they are remembered as more accomplished, beautiful, and generous than they ever were in life. Joseph was a great guy, to be sure, but in Jacob's mind he must have reached incredible new heights.

The brothers had gotten rid of Joseph, but they couldn't erase him from their father's memory. The tension in the home must have been palpable as they offered Jacob insincere condolences and continued to cover their sin. I wonder if any of them was tempted to break down and tell the truth. Perhaps they tried to ease their guilt with thoughts like, *"We didn't really lie; we just found the coat—of course, we found it on Joseph's back. And, we didn't actually tell Dad Joseph was dead; we just gave him the bloody coat, and he reached his own conclusions."* Those twenty pieces of silver probably didn't seem like such a bargain, after all. This was yet one more time when things could have been made right if the brothers had confessed their sin.

Running Away from Home
Without pausing for the chapter break, please read Genesis 37:34–38:1. (In its original form, the Bible did not have chapter and verse divisions; they were added later for convenience in looking up passages.)

Given the circumstances at home, can you think why Judah may have wanted to move to Adullum?

_____

_____

_____

The timing of Judah's departure makes it likely that as organizer of the plan to sell Joseph, he wanted to get away from any reminder of what he'd done. But if Judah wanted to hide from God and run from guilt, he was trying to achieve the impossible, for we can never conceal ourselves or our sin from the Lord. The Bible says, *"Where can I go from Your Spirit? Or where can I flee from Your presence?"* (Psalm 139:7).

Can you think of other ways people try to run or hide from God besides physically?

_____

_____

_____

Judah's behavior is a common reaction of those trying to escape. I've known individuals like him who habitually run from their problems, leaving others in their wake. They move to a different location, flit from one relationship to another, frequently change jobs, or hop from church to church. Others try to hide from God by denying His existence. After all, if there is no God, then there is no judgment, no accounting for behavior. I can do what I want; I am my own judge.

APPLY Describe a time when you tried to run or hide from God.

_____

_____

_____

_____

Adullum was less than a day's walk from home—close enough for family contact if Judah desired, but far enough he didn't have to listen to his father's lamenting. Whatever his motivation for leaving home, Judah's brothers were left to deal with the problems he helped create. But while it appears Judah was running *from* the consequences of his actions, he was actually running *toward* Jesus the Messiah.

Genesis 37 ends with Joseph being sold to Potiphar, and picks up again in Genesis 39. Genesis 38 almost seems to have been added with no connection to Joseph's story. It begins with Judah leaving home, and then details his relationship with Tamar and the twin boys born as a result of his and her union.

What were the names of Tamar and Judah's sons (Genesis 38:29, 30)?

_____

Whose genealogy begins in Matthew 1:1?

_____

_____

What four characters named in Matthew 1:3 are also named in Genesis 38?

_____

_____

Genesis 38 is not a break in the narrative, but merely a step showing us how Judah and Tamar became part of the direct lineage of the Messiah. Their story is not only an integral part of Joseph's, but becomes our story, too, for we become part of the covenant blessing when we put our faith in Jesus as Savior. God gave the covenant promises to Abraham to be carried on

"I acknowledged my sin to You, And my iniquity I did not hide; I said, "I will confess my transgressions to the LORD"; And You forgave the guilt of my sin. Selah."

Psalm 32:5

through Isaac, Jacob, the twelve brothers, and ultimately the Jewish nation of Israel. But of all the brothers, Judah was the one chosen to be in the Messiah's lineage.

I don't know why God chose to bring us Jesus through Judah; to be honest, I would have picked Joseph. Yet once again we see the grace and mercy and forgiveness of God as He works in the lives of people, in spite of their failings.

I Didn't Apply for This Job

DAY TWO

GET ME OUT OF HERE: THIS ISN'T WHERE I WANT TO LIVE!

Pray this verse: *"Open my eyes, that I may behold Wonderful things from Your law."* (Psalm 119:18)

As a young child, I was quite content living in the Minnesota culture and environment into which I had been born. But when I was nine years old, I moved with my mother and two stepbrothers from the Twin Cities to the Florida Keys. Until the moment we were packed into the car I had no inkling we were moving. I didn't want to go. I didn't want to leave my home, my friends, my father, and my other siblings. I didn't want to once again be the "new" kid (I would be starting my fourth school in four years). The southern climate and customs were foreign to me. My new school was segregated, and my classmates spoke with an accent. The island on which we lived was barely three blocks wide and the population of our town a mere twelve hundred. There were daily rain showers, and the humidity made my sheets feel damp when I crawled into bed. Believe me, it was a long time before I could call Florida my home.

The people in Egypt spoke an unfamiliar language, wrote with a peculiar alphabet, ate strange foods, wore unusual clothing and hairstyles, and lived in dwellings unlike any Joseph had ever seen.

That childhood transition was difficult, but consider Joseph's move to Egypt—the emotional, physical, and spiritual devastation! His own brothers had betrayed and nearly killed him, he was shackled and bruised during the journey, and now he would spend the rest of his life in a pagan nation—not even as an average citizen, but as a lowly slave. Imagine his bewilderment as he took in his surroundings. The people spoke an unfamiliar language and wrote with a peculiar alphabet; ate strange foods; wore unusual clothing and hairstyles; and lived in dwellings unlike those of Joseph's seminomadic upbringing. His life was completely cut off from all he had known, with no hope of contact or reconciliation with his loved ones. His possessions back home would have been few by today's standards, but he was unable to take even one personal item with him. He had nothing; even the coat on his back had been stripped away. To say Joseph experienced a culture shock would be a big understatement.

Emotional Adjustments
Reading through Genesis might give one the impression Joseph was like Mary Poppins—practically perfect in every way. He was an extraordinary young man, but he had his struggles and weaknesses, too.

📖 Read Genesis 41:50–52.

In Week Two we learned that children were named for specific reasons during Bible times. The names of Joseph's sons give us insight into some of his mental and emotional struggles during his first thirteen years in Egypt. He named his first son *Manasseh* (Hebrew: *M^enashsheh*), meaning "causing to forget" because God had helped him to forget his "trouble" (`*amal*), meaning "toil, wearing effort, worry," whether of body or mind. His second son was named *Ephraim* (Hebrew: *'Ephrayim*), meaning "double fruit" because God made him fruitful in the "land of my affliction" (`*oniy*), meaning "depression" as in misery or trouble.

What do the meanings of Joseph's sons' names tell you about his emotional struggles and state of mind during his years of slavery?

_____

_____

_____

Word Study
DOUBLE TROUBLE

Manasseh means "causing to forget."

The Hebrew word translated "trouble" in Genesis 41:50–52 implies "toil, wearing effort, worry."

Ephraim means "double fruit."

The Hebrew word translated "affliction" in this same passage suggests "depression," as in misery or trouble.

Joseph was just like you and me. He worried about his circumstances, and battled emotional fatigue. He struggled with depression, and at times he was just plain miserable. I think we sometimes give and/or get the impression Christians are always, or should be, joyful, and that there's something wrong if we get discouraged or downcast. It would be wonderful if we were always upbeat, but it's just not reality! We all face emotional challenges, and sometimes we handle them better than at other times. The Christian life is not about pretending you're thrilled with your trials or where you're living, and it's not about suppressing your feelings. It's about acknowledging your struggles and emotions, then trusting and serving the Lord in spite of them, and that's what Joseph did.

The Bible records the fears and emotions of many other spiritual heroes:

- Queen Esther (Esther 4 and 5) was scared to death (almost literally) to go before the king with her request. But she prayed and moved ahead in faith.

- King David was discouraged and/or depressed in many of the psalms he wrote. But he prayed and moved ahead in faith.

- The apostle Paul struggled to be joyful and content in prison (Philippians 1). But he prayed and moved ahead in faith.

- Even Jesus revealed His emotions as He wept after the death of Lazarus and anguished in the Garden of Gethsemane before His death. But He prayed and moved ahead in faith.

After Manasseh and Ephraim were born, they were daily reminders of God's love and faithfulness. Through them, Joseph acknowledged his struggles with misery, worry, and depression, but he didn't live his life waiting for circumstances to change. Perhaps you've gone through a difficult relocation experience and you're trying to find contentment with your job, salary, home, climate, church, or friends. Perhaps your present locality was not of your own choosing. Okay, let's stop right here! Whether you realize it or not, God is directing your "caravan" just as He did Joseph's; He is still in control. Though your caravan may be stopped somewhere not to your liking, God has a special purpose for you right where you are. He is concerned about what happens to you; He is listening to your prayers; He cares about your feelings. You don't yet know the end of your story—but God does.

Describe a time when you were discontent with your location, job, etc. Looking back, how do you see God preparing you for His special purpose?

_____

_____

_____

_____

Have I Got a Job for You!
Read 2 Corinthians 5:17–21.

What message does God entrust to Christians (v. 19)?

_____

_____

_____

To what position are we appointed (v. 20)?

_____

_____

_____

The Greek word translated "ambassador" (*presbeuo*) means to be a "senior," by implication to act as a representative. Although Joseph didn't have the New Testament as a reference, I believe he understood he was Jehovah's representative in Egypt. We, too, are ambassadors for Jehovah, the King of kings, the Lord of lords, right where we are. He has appointed you and me to represent Him and to share with the world His message of reconciliation through faith in Jesus Christ.

An ambassador:
- represents the king's purposes and standards through speech and actions.
- stands in place of the king in a foreign country.
- must be in a state of readiness to be called home (to heaven) at any time.
- seeks the interests of the king, not his or her own.
- does not take criticism personally.
- is protected by the king.
- is provided for by the king.

When I picture myself as God's representative it completely changes my perspective about my life and circumstances, and it will yours, too. We are official ambassadors right now, right in our homes, cities, churches, jobs, and families. We have a position no else can fill; we can touch lives no one else can touch; we have a purpose no one can accomplish but us. Our location is designated by God—He has directed our "caravans" for His purpose.

> **God has appointed us to represent Him and to share with the world His message of reconciliation through faith in Jesus Christ.**

 List some practical ways you can be an ambassador for Christ in your present location and circumstances.

_____

_____

_____

_____

Note how each of the following verses can help us grow in contentment in our location and/or circumstances:

Philippians 1:12–21

_____

_____

_____

Philippians 4:11–13, 19

_____

_____

_____

1 Timothy 6:6–12

_____

_____

_____

Hebrews 13:5, 6

_____

_____

_____

Discontentment generally comes when:
• we don't get our own way.
• we want what someone else has.
• we compare our circumstances with those of others, thinking those folks are better off than we are.

Chuck Swindoll says he believes life is 10 percent what happens to us and 90 percent how we react to it, and I agree. Contentment in location and circumstances is largely based on attitude, and as difficult as it may be to make, attitude is a conscious choice.

I Wasn't Raised to Be a Slave

In Genesis 39, Joseph really begins to show what kind of man he is. No doubt, he had some maturing to do and some attitude adjustments to make, and probably the trauma of the pit and being sold into slavery contributed to that process. But, I believe that because he had been a *boy* of integrity and character, Joseph showed himself to be a *man* of integrity and character in the subsequent years.

A Slave in Egypt

Try to picture Joseph's surroundings, his physical condition, and emotional state of mind when he arrived in Egypt. Write your thoughts below.

_____

_____

_____

_____

After a journey of at least two weeks, and more than two hundred miles, trudging along in shackles, Joseph had to be exhausted, dirty, thin, bruised, and sore. He must have felt rejection and loss over his past and fears about his future as he was paraded in humiliation before potential buyers haggling in a strange tongue. Perhaps he was thinking, _I don't belong here; this is all wrong; I belong in my father's tents and in the fields minding the flocks._ He may have looked out over the crowd, hoping and praying his brothers had decided to rescue him, after all. Or maybe he considered escape. But a man could die trying to cross that great expanse of desert by himself.

From a human perspective, Joseph's life might have seemed over. He was in a strange, pagan country, forced into a job he didn't want to do. He could have no expectation for any sort of normal life—a wife and children; a home of his own; an eventual change in jobs. He was starting at the bottom of the employment chain, and the only promotion he'd ever get would be from insignificant slave with no pay to insignificant slave with more responsibility and still no pay.

But Joseph's life wasn't over—in a sense, his real purpose was just beginning. Let's see how he handled this seemingly hopeless situation.

📖 Read Genesis 37:36 and 39:1.

Who bought Joseph from the Ishmaelites?

_____

_____

_____

What was Potiphar's position in Pharaoh's court?

_____

_____

_____

As a court official, Potiphar would be among the upper classes, owning land and a nice home, and knowledgeable of palace happenings.

📖 Read Genesis 39:2–6.

Who was _with_ Joseph (v. 2)?

_____

_____

Word Study
NAMES OF GOD

Names of God in Hebrew:

- God ('elohiym) – (plural) specifically used of the supreme God
- Lord ('Adonay) – a title of God meaning Lord or Master
- LORD (Yehovah) – Jehovah, Jewish national name of God

I love this verse. Did you know this is the first time since Joseph's birth in which God is explicitly cited in Scripture in direct relation to Joseph (Genesis 30:24)? I find that remarkable! God's fingerprints are all over Joseph's story in Genesis 37, and we know He watched over the young man in the pit and guided his caravan, yet He was never specifically mentioned. Genesis 39 clearly confirms that God was *with* Joseph in Potiphar's household, and to substantiate that point, the verse says *"the LORD"* was with him. LORD spelled with all capital letters in the Old Testament refers to God's personal name—*Jehovah*. When all human hope had failed, Jehovah was *personally with* Joseph!

Look at Genesis 39:2 once again. What resulted in Jehovah being with Joseph?

_____

_____

_____

Depending on your translation, the Bible says Joseph was "successful" or "prosperous." Don't you find it odd a lowly slave with no foreseeable future was considered by God to be successful/prosperous? Only the Lord could make a statement like that, because His definition of success, or prosperity, is not the same as ours. His definition is for us to be where He wants us to be, doing what He wants us to do—simple obedience.

I'm encouraged by the implications of that verse for my own life. It's akin to the Lord saying to me, "I understand when you go through difficult times; I know you don't always feel like your ministry is successful; I know you sometimes feel like a slave to your circumstances, but *I am with you*. You are a success; you are prosperous, because you're exactly where I want you to be, doing what I want you to do."

According to verse 3, what did Potiphar see in Joseph's life?

_____

_____

What position was given to Joseph as a result of his diligent service?

_____

_____

Why did God bless Potiphar?

_____

_____

Joseph had lived a seminomadic existence; life in a city was completely alien to him. Yet he worked hard and learned how to run an Egyptian household, becoming skilled in writing and fluent in the language. He became personal attendant to Potiphar and eventually rose above the other slaves to be overseer of the entire household *and* the fields. But greater than that, in an unbelieving household, in a pagan nation that worshipped hundreds of gods, Joseph's work ethic was such that Potiphar attributed his outstanding productivity to Jehovah.

> *"For He Himself has said, 'I WILL NEVER DESERT YOU, NOR WILL I EVER FORSAKE YOU.'"*
>
> **Hebrews 13:5b**

> *Joseph didn't feel he was too good for the job of a slave; he was simply good at the job of a slave.*

📖 Read Ephesians 6:5–8.

These verses could easily have been written with Joseph in mind. He made a point of being the best servant in the house, whether or not his master was a believer, and there is no indication he felt any humiliation in, or resentment at, being a slave.

How do you measure up in your position of employment? Answer the following questions. (If you are not presently employed in the workplace, think back to your last paid position working under management.)

Do you serve your boss as conscientiously as you would serve Christ, whether or not he or she is a believer?

_____

_____

_____

Do you work diligently and with integrity, *especially* when no one is looking?

_____

_____

_____

Do others give credit to the Lord because you're a capable worker on the job; in your home; in the community?

_____

_____

_____

Are you respectful, or do you criticize your boss behind his or her back?

_____

_____

_____

Does God bless *others* because of the work you do?

_____

_____

_____

Joseph had on-the-job training in Potiphar's household, but can you think how his home life might have prepared him as well?

_____

_____

_____

Joseph had been trained at home for his new position, and he didn't even know it. By the time he became a part of Potiphar's household he had already been in leadership training under his father. He knew how to provide for a large household, manage immense herds and flocks, and, no doubt, handle business transactions and keep accounting records. Growing up in a large family, Joseph also learned to deal with various personalities and temperaments, and his life as a semi-nomadic shepherd taught him to endure the physical hardships of harsh weather, rugged terrain, and dangerous animals.

 As you look back over your life, can you see how God has prepared you for your present position at home, at work, in the community, or at church? Please explain.

_____

_____

_____

_____

Joseph is a marvelous example of a servant, but we have an even better model in Jesus Christ.

📖 Please read Philippians 2:5–11.

I'm in awe that the God of the universe humbly came to Earth to serve me and endure the shame of the cross to save me. How could I ever feel humiliation in any job or position He calls me to do? Jesus the Son, who is exalted above all, came to serve and sacrifice and love. He is everything, yet He made himself nothing. He was humbly obedient as He took on the form of a slave to fulfill the Father's plan.

📖 Read Colossians 3:22–24.

I believe that Joseph understood that, although he was working in Potiphar's home, he was actually serving God. He served with sincerity of heart, not just trying to please a man, but pleasing the Lord and knowing that his reward would come from Him. He was truly freer as a captive slave than his brothers were in their so-called freedom at home. They were bound by sin and guilt; Joseph was freed by God's love and grace.

CHOOSING TO OBEY WHEN GOD DOESN'T MAKE SENSE

Pray this verse: *"Open my eyes, that I may behold Wonderful things from Your law."* (Psalm 119:18)

Obedience is a choice. And it's a fairly easy one when our jobs are secure, the bills are paid, we have our health, and our relationships are going well. Then, God is good, life is great, and serving Him makes perfect sense. But what about when God leads our caravan on an uncertain path—one that doesn't make sense? Do we still choose obedience?

Becoming a good leader first requires becoming a good servant.

"For even the Son of Man did not come to be served, but to serve, and to give His life a ransom for many."

Mark 10:45

I Didn't Apply for This Job

DAY FOUR

In Joseph's case, his brothers hated him and wished he were dead, he was stuck in a city where he didn't want to live and with a job he didn't want. He had no friends, and his future seemed hopeless. So, was God still good? Did serving Him still make sense?

Yes, God was still good, and though Joseph didn't know how his future would resolve itself, he entrusted it to the Lord and chose obedience. He didn't wait for his circumstances to change or for his prayers to be answered his way. From our perspective his choices were wise and sensible, because once again, we know the end of the story, and we know why and how God was working in his life. For all Joseph knew, he would be a lowly slave for the rest of his life.

I trusted Christ as my Savior more than forty years ago, and since that time, I've watched many of my friends and acquaintances live a mediocre Christian life, and in some cases give up all together. Oh, they still believe in Jesus as their Savior, but because of disappointing circumstances or hardships they've lost their passion for serving the Lord and have chosen a life of selective obedience—obeying when the circumstances are right.

APPLY Have you ever purposefully chosen to *not* obey the Lord? Why? Can you think of reasons why others might make a similar choice?

_____

_____

_____

_____

Your list may include the death of a loved one, a broken romance, financial setbacks, a shattered dream, the temptations of the world, or other situations. And who do people sometimes blame for those disappointments? Why, God, of course. He could have or should have intervened and made everything all right. He let us down; He allowed a child to die; He didn't answer our prayers. If hardship, suffering, and heartache are what serving the Lord means, it isn't worth it, we might think.

But I've come to realize God's ways *shouldn't* always make sense to me. It's why God is God, and I'm not. It's what faith is all about—not understanding the reasons why, but *knowing* I can trust Him and that what He's doing is best for me because He loves me. It's believing He is directing my caravan over the bumps and ruts, and that He knows the end of my path. It's knowing that, even when I can't see the light at the end of the tunnel, I can still see Him.

We don't always need to know God's purpose; we only need to know He has a purpose.

I think Joseph believed those truths, and chose to obey even when his life was utterly disappointing and unfair. There's no indication in the Bible that God ever appeared to Joseph as He had his forefathers, or spoke to him and told him to hang in there because in thirteen years everything would be okay. He only had two dreams he didn't understand and the testimony of his ancestors to hang on to. And yet, it made sense to Joseph to be obedient.

Each of the following Scripture passages has been a great help to me in understanding why it's impossible to comprehend God's mind and purposes.

They have truly helped to increase my faith. Take a moment to let each passage speak to you. After each verse, record your thoughts.

Psalm 42:11

_____

_____

Isaiah 55:8, 9

_____

_____

Romans 8:28, 35–39

_____

_____

Romans 15:4–6

_____

_____

Ephesians 3:14–21

_____

_____

> **"Why are you downcast, O my soul? Why so disturbed within me? Put your hope in God, for I will yet praise him, my Savior and my God."**
>
> **Psalm 42:11 (NIV)**

When You Don't _Feel_ Like Obeying

I'm a night person, and I don't always _feel_ like getting up in the morning; I don't always _feel_ like cleaning my house; I rarely _feel_ like cooking. I'll even admit I don't always _feel_ like going to church, reading my Bible, and having my prayer time. But, I do those things because it's right, and when I do, my attitude nearly always changes in a positive way.

Let's be honest—sometimes disobedience can feel pretty good. Even the Bible says there's pleasure in sin for a short time (Hebrews 11:25). But neither our obedience nor disobedience should be dependent upon our feelings. I doubt Joseph always _felt_ like doing the right thing. In fact, I'm sure there were times he reacted on an emotional level, just as do you and I. But for the most part, Joseph did the right thing in spite of his circumstances and feelings.

Fortunately, the Lord understands struggles between doing right and doing wrong, and that feelings and emotions can influence us. However, we're to control _them_, not let them control _us_.

Read Galatians 5:16–25.

What two things are in opposition to each other (v. 17)?

_____

_____

What are the deeds of the flesh, or sinful nature (vv. 19–21)?

_____

_____

What are the acts, or fruit, of the Spirit (vv. 22, 23)?

_____

_____

_____

Did You Know?
HOLY SPIRIT INDWELLING

Joseph did not have the same advantage we have today. During Old Testament times the Holy Spirit did not permanently indwell believers.

All of us are born with a sinful nature (also referred to as "the old nature," "the flesh," "the old man")—it's why we do things that are wrong. When we trust Christ as our Savior we are indwelt by the Holy Spirit, who gives us a new nature ("the new birth," "the new man") and the power to be obedient and do what is right. But, those two natures are in conflict, and as long as we're on Earth, our old nature will battle against our new nature and we will struggle to be obedient. It's our job to strengthen the new nature through obedience so the conflict will not be as great. Thankfully, that sinful nature will have no part in our home in heaven.

APPLY Describe a time when you had a conflict between your old and new natures.

_____

_____

_____

_____

📖 Please read 1 Corinthians 15:57, 58.

Who has won the victory for us?

_____

_____

What does God guarantee about the work we do for Him?

_____

_____

_____

📖 Now read Galatians 6:9, 10.

If we don't give up, what will happen?

_____

_____

_____

"So then, those who suffer according to God's will should commit themselves to their faithful Creator and continue to do good."

1 Peter 4:19 (NIV)

You may feel just like Joseph—trapped in your circumstances with no way of escape and no light at the end of your tunnel. Don't give up! God has a purpose for you, and He will reveal it to you at the right time. Joseph could have given in to feelings of despair and hopelessness, but instead he patiently endured and God eventually used him in almost unbelievable ways.

When God doesn't make sense to us, we need to focus on His faithfulness and remember His marvelous deeds. Joseph knew that the Lord had been faithful to his ancestors; he knew about the covenant promises; he knew that God had guided his caravan. He knew the Lord hadn't changed, and if He could be trusted in the past, He could be trusted for the present and the future.

I know it's not easy to serve God when it seems He doesn't hear your prayers or when your circumstances don't improve in spite of your faithfulness. I know some of you are experiencing unimaginable pain and heartache. I don't have an answer that will solve your problems, but I do have a God who loves you and cares about what you're going through and wants to lead your caravan even though your path is filled with obstacles. I am praying for you, my friend.

FOR ME TO FOLLOW GOD

I Didn't Apply for This Job

DAY FIVE

Pray this verse: *"Open my eyes, that I may behold Wonderful things from Your law."* (Psalm 119:18)

I am directionally challenged. In other words, I get lost. Just ask my family. If you give me directions, do not include *north, south, east,* or *west;* those words mean absolutely nothing to me. You need to say right or left, the number of blocks or miles I need to drive, and for good measure, throw in a landmark or two. When I travel I have a road map, directions from the Internet, a GPS navigational system, *and* I always carry my cell phone.

In order to follow God, we need directional tools, too. Perhaps you feel as if you're stuck at a roadside rest stop, waiting to get back on the highway. Maybe you're going in circles, and you keep hearing an annoying voice (like my GPS) say "recalculating." In a very real sense we do have the tools we need—the Bible is better than a road map, the Holy Spirit is more reliable than a GPS, and our prayers never have dropped calls as does a cell phone. The problem is we don't like waiting for instructions, and we don't always want to follow them when we do get them.

Let's take a look at a few characters from this week's study. After each name, note the direction you think his caravan was headed.

Judah

_____

_____

Jacob

_____

_____

Joseph

_____

_____

I think of Judah as being on a *detour*. He tried to run from the consequences of his sinful decisions, yet he could not run from God's plan for his life, and for all of mankind. Some detours are of our own making, like Judah's, and some are sent directly from God, like Joseph's. If we're detouring away from God, we need to stop and work our way back to His path. If God has put us on a detour, we need to accept that path, seek His guidance, and proceed with caution.

Jacob was at a *rest stop*. God had confirmed to him the Abrahamic covenant—he would become a great nation and all the world would be blessed through him, but it would be twenty-two years before he would see that promise begin to become a reality.

Joseph was *right on course*. He may not have *felt* like it, and he may not have *liked* it, but he was exactly where God wanted him. His circumstances were out of his control, leaving him with two choices: Wallow in grief and depression, or obey in faith and take one step at a time.

 What about you? Circle where you think your caravan is on your journey.

Detour   Rest Stop   Right on course

Explain your answer.

_____

_____

_____

In truth, whether you're on a detour or at a rest stop, you still might be right on course. Look at Joseph. He didn't *plan* on becoming a slave in Egypt, but God took him there on a detour. He didn't *plan* on accompanying a caravan to Egypt, but he was right on course. He didn't *plan* on waiting thirteen years to understand the reason why, but God was preparing him at a rest stop.

Could God have fulfilled His plan in another way—done something easier, less traumatic, or less heartbreaking for Joseph? Of course, He *could* have, but He allows us to make our own choices and decisions, and sometimes the consequences are painful. Joseph's brothers made some sinful decisions and everyone suffered as a result. Yet God still continued to work in their lives, and before our study is through, we'll see that those men were transformed.

📖 Please read Romans 12:1, 2.

What does God find acceptable (v.1)?

_____

_____

Transformation will result in what?

_____

_____

_____

Transformation is the process of renewing our minds, which ultimately results in our doing God's will. That process can be slow, but our patient heavenly Father delights in that very thing. In other words, the actual *process* of our spiritual growth through developing faith, obedience, and godly char-

Don't miss the blessing of the journey because you are only looking for the end result.

acter is what brings glory to Him; the *process* is what makes us into the men and women He wants us to be. Potiphar watched that process in Joseph, and that's why he recognized the hand of God in the young man's life.

APPLY How do you see God transforming your life?

_____

_____

_____

Would you consider yourself content with your present location?

_____

_____

_____

List five character qualities you can develop by remaining where you are (e.g., patience, humility, perseverance).

_____

_____

_____

What Does It Mean to Be a Servant?

Read the following Scriptures, then describe what you think characterizes a godly servant.

John 12:25, 26

_____

_____

_____

Romans 12:1, 3, 10, 11

_____

_____

_____

1 Corinthians 9:19–23

_____

_____

_____

Galatians 1:10

_____

_____

_____

My husband and I have worked in church leadership for more than thirty years, and I've observed three types of servants in every ministry:

> *You may not be able to change your location, but you can change your attitude.*

1. Selective Service – These folks say they want to serve, but they don't really want to be a servant. In other words, they like giving an *impression* of godliness and service by taking high-profile positions, but they don't want to get their hands dirty with jobs that don't get the glory.

2. Silent Service – These are the people who have faithfully served for many years, then decide it's time to sit back and be a spectator. They no longer come to church to give, but for what they can get. They say things like, "I put my time in [in the nursery, teaching Sunday School, being a deacon, or . . .], let someone younger do it now."

3. Sacrificial Service – These are the people willing to step out of their comfort zone and do what needs to be done, and they don't seek accolades for doing it. They'll shovel the snow, clean up after potluck dinners, and wash the toilets. And when they're done with all that they'll change diapers in the nursery, teach a Sunday school class, and serve on a board if needed.

APPLY Which kind of servant are you? Circle one. Explain.

Selective Service   Silent Service   Sacrificial Service

_____

_____

_____

The Object of Joseph's Passion
A few years ago a friend of mine asked me my passion. I thought for a moment, then named several things I'm passionate about. Later, I realized she was asking what *drives* me, what motivates me to do what I do, and I revised my answer.

So, let me ask you the same question. What is your passion? Who is your passion? Is it your job, your mate, your hobby, your children? What is it that drives you? What is it that keeps you going?

_____

_____

_____

_____

God was Joseph's driving passion. It's what kept him going when literally everything he had—family, home, hopes, dreams, clothes—had been taken away from him. He had nothing but the Lord, but found he *needed* nothing but the Lord. He was content to use his life to bring honor and glory to the Lord by serving others.

I wish I could say Jesus is *always* my driving passion. But too often I become consumed with success, money, possessions, hobbies, and even other people. There's nothing wrong with those things; in fact, each of them can find an appropriate place in our lives. But, when any of those becomes the object of our passion, our focus turns inward, and we will eventually be discouraged, disappointed, or hurt, and we will no longer be an effective servant. When people and things are our focus, the problems and their solutions become

In God's service, there is no retirement.

"But seek first His kingdom and His righteousness; and all these things will be added to you."

Matthew 6:33

our worries and concerns. However, when God becomes our driving passion, our focus will be on souls, eternity, praise, worship, obedience, and service to others, and our worries and concerns become *His*.

 Heavenly Father, Sometimes I'm confused about where my caravan is headed; I sometimes seem to be on a detour or waiting at a rest stop. But wherever You choose to place me, I want to be right on course and content to be there. Please make Your directions and instructions clear to me. Forgive me when I become focused on things instead of Jesus; I want to keep my eyes on Him; I want to be an effective servant for You. In Jesus' name I pray, amen.

Joseph had nothing but the Lord; he needed nothing but the Lord.

Notes

5

Walking by Faith—Again!

Welcome to Week Five. Can you believe it? We're already halfway through our study. I hope you're beginning to love Joseph's story as much as I do, and that you've had some new insights into your own life as a result of delving into his.

Can you imagine your life in print like Abraham's, Isaac's, Jacob's, and the twelve brothers? If my life were more like Joseph's, perhaps I wouldn't mind, but I've made many foolish decisions I don't want in print. The good thing is we can learn from each other's mistakes, as well as the triumphs.

When we study the lives of the great men and women of the Bible, the tendency is to think, *Yeah, but that was then and this is now* or, *But my situation is so much worse than his (or hers).* Your circumstances may seem to be worse than Joseph's, but they are not bigger than God—there is nothing He can't handle.

Now, let's get to it. Joseph has barely arrived in Egypt, and we have a lot of ground to cover. This week we'll see him betrayed, wrongly accused, forsaken, and thrown into prison!

It's Not Just a Job–It's a Ministry

Pray this verse: *"Open my eyes, that I may behold Wonderful things from Your law."* (Psalm 119:18)

We used to shop at a Wal-Mart near our home in South Florida. An older gentleman sat near the entrance and said, "Welcome to Wal-Mart" as you entered and, "Thank you for shopping at Wal-Mart" as you left the store. My kids used to love to imitate his deep, gravelly voice. The man obviously loved his job, and he did it well. He was such a character that, not only did he make you glad you came to shop, but he made you want to work there! I have no idea if the man was a Christian, but intentional or not, his post at that door wasn't just a job; it was a ministry.

That Wal-Mart greeter made a lasting impression on me, and though I probably saw his name tag a hundred times, I couldn't tell you now what it said. He wasn't a highly paid executive; he probably held one of the lowliest positions in the store. He was never going to be promoted, and he will not be remembered throughout the world. But, he enjoyed his job, he liked to make people happy, and he was good for the company. And, fifteen years later, I still can picture his face and hear the sound of his voice in my mind.

You, too, make an impression on those with whom you work or otherwise come in contact. The question is whether it's positive or negative. I don't know what your job is—homemaker, teacher, police officer, pastor, executive, trash collector, or any of hundreds of others—but you have the prospect of ministering to others.

When you hear the word *minister* you probably think of a pastor or priest. However, the verb *minister* is defined as "to give aid or service"; in other words, anyone can minister. Joseph gave service and aid to his master; he *ministered* while doing his job. He wasn't an employee by our modern definition; he was a slave by force. And, that's all the more reason why we can learn from his model behavior.

APPLY Before we look at today's text in more detail, I'd like you to answer a few questions about your job. Be completely honest.

What do you like most about your job?

_____

_____

_____

What do you like least about your job?

_____

_____

_____

Are you content in your employment?

_____

_____

Would you work harder if you were paid more or had better benefits?

_____

_____

_____

Do you ever misuse time?

_____

_____

_____

Do you work harder when others are watching?

_____

_____

How would your boss rate your job performance?

_____

_____

If you are the boss, how would your employees rate your job performance?

_____

_____

_____

Do you believe the Lord is pleased with your work ethic?

_____

_____

_____

📖 Please read Genesis 39:1–6.

If anyone had cause to be bitter or angry about his job, it was Joseph. List some reasons he might have resented his position as a slave.

_____

_____

_____

Before Joseph was promoted to overseer, he had to learn a new form of writing and language, and the workings of an Egyptian household, and gain the respect of Potiphar. He could have given less effort to his work, having concluded life wasn't fair, God didn't answer his prayers, he was overqualified, or there was no room for advancement. Those thoughts may have passed through his mind, but he didn't let them linger, and he didn't sit around waiting for his circumstances to change.

Genesis 39:2 sets the stage for the rest of Joseph's life: "*The LORD was with Joseph . . .*" What a comforting assurance! "In all of Joseph's troubles, his secret power was in his consciousness of the presence of God."[1]

"The LORD is near to all who call upon Him, To all who call upon Him in truth."

Psalm 145:18

Verse 3 also says Joseph prospered (was successful), which is obvious by the fact that Potiphar promoted him, but I think there's more to that thought. The Hebrew word *tsalach* means "to push forward, come (mightily), be profitable." Success didn't just happen for Joseph—he worked at it; he *pushed forward*; he was a *profitable* laborer.

According to verse 3, of what was Potiphar aware?

_____

_____

_____

Remember that the Egyptians were pagans, worshipping hundreds of gods, yet Potiphar knew that Jehovah was the driving force in Joseph's life. Whatever Joseph said to Potiphar, he backed it up with his actions. He conducted his life in such a way others recognized the hand of God and were not offended by the way he shared his faith.

I've known Christians who have gone to both extremes in sharing their faith on the job—some never said a word, and others wouldn't shut up. If your job doesn't allow you to speak about Christ, then don't do it (or get another job). If you have the freedom to share, please do; but don't be offensive, and don't keep talking when you've said enough. Either way, your conduct should speak just as loud as your words.

📖 Read Genesis 39:4. Why did Joseph become Potiphar's personal attendant?

_____

_____

_____

> **"Only conduct yourselves in a manner worthy of the gospel of Christ."**
>
> **Philippians 1:27a**

Joseph began as just another slave, but Potiphar saw that the Lord was with him and promoted him to be his personal servant and eventually overseer of all his properties.

What might Joseph's responsibilities have been as:

Potiphar's personal attendant?

_____

_____

Overseer of Potiphar's household and fields?

_____

_____

Genesis 39:4 (NKJV) says, "So Joseph found favor in his sight, and served him." The Hebrew word translated "served" (*sharath*) in verse 4 (NKJV) means "to attend, contribute" as in ministering, waiting on. Joseph was diligent as he attended and ministered to Potiphar. Is it any wonder Joseph found favor in this powerful Egyptian's sight?

📖 Read Genesis 39:5.

Have you ever sat back and watched someone else reap the rewards after you've done all the work? Normally, this is the complete opposite of what we would consider a blessing. *We* want to reap the rewards; *we* want to have the success; *we* want to experience the prosperity from our efforts. Joseph was learning that God's idea of a blessing isn't the same as ours. He worked hard, honored the Lord, and *Potiphar's* household and financial holdings were blessed. But, glorifying God by serving, *really serving*, others was the most important thing in Joseph's life. It was more important to him that others were blessed than that he himself was blessed.

APPLY Have you learned to rejoice and be content when others are blessed, successful, and prosperous because of your hard work?

_____

_____

_____

According to Genesis 39:6, what did Potiphar entrust to Joseph?

_____

_____

With what did Potiphar concern himself?

_____

_____

_____

Although we don't know Joseph's precise age when he was promoted by Potiphar, he would still have been quite a young man. Additionally, he was a foreigner with no special credentials. Yet, because he proved himself to be honest, devoted, and responsible, Potiphar entrusted all he owned to him and had no concerns for what went on in his household or in his fields. Joseph's responsibilities would have included handling the finances, buying provisions for the home, managing the crops, and supervising the other slaves.

APPLY Can you be trusted on the job? Does your employer have to watch so you don't waste time? Do you manage well what has been entrusted to you?

_____

_____

_____

As we close today's lesson, please look up the following Scripture passages. Although they primarily refer to the position of a slave, we can make a secondary application to employment. After each verse note the attributes of a good laborer.

Ephesians 6:5, 6

_____

_____

The question should not be whether God is blessing you, but whether others are being blessed because of you.

Joseph was shrewd, faithful, and loyal with everything entrusted to him.

Colossians 3:22–24

_____

_____

1 Timothy 6:1, 2

_____

_____

Titus 2:9, 10

_____

_____

Worshipping God When Those Around You Don't

Pray this verse: *"Open my eyes, that I may behold Wonderful things from Your law."* (Psalm 119:18)

Did You Know?

PHARAOHS OF EGYPT

The pharaohs were believed to be gods, and thus had vast power and authority.

When Joseph moved to Egypt he was leaving more than just his family and a familiar culture; he was leaving his religious heritage and those with whom he could freely worship. Even with all the family turmoil in the home, at least they all believed in the same God and could worship Him in freedom. But, the Egyptians were polytheistic, worshipping hundreds of gods, some human, some animal, some a combination of human and animal. The pharaohs were also believed to be gods, and thus had vast power and authority. There were no community services in the temples, for the temples were reserved for the priests to present daily offerings and other gifts to the gods. By virtue of their position, the priests had immense control and influence over the common people, who paid homage in their homes to idols representing the deity(ies) of their choice.

Certainly Joseph knew such cultures existed and had seen them on a smaller scale, but to live among people who did not acknowledge his God was completely new to him. He had grown up listening to the stories of the Creation, the Flood, and Abraham and Isaac, and he knew that his family was part of God's plan for the redemption of the world. Joseph had seen his father build altars in the wilderness, and he understood the concept of being able to worship the Lord anytime and anyplace. He believed all power and glory belonged to Jehovah, not to a man or gods created in the mind of man. As a descendant of Abraham, Joseph knew that God had a plan for his life in spite of his circumstances and surroundings, and he was determined to live a life of faith that honored and glorified God.

If you live in the United States, you can probably find a place to worship with like-minded believers within a reasonable driving distance of your home. In some areas, it might be a bit more difficult, but for the most part we don't have to worship alone. That fellowship will usually meet on Sundays and for a midweek Bible study or two, but what do you do when those with whom you work or live on a daily basis don't share your faith? What do you do when your beliefs are repeatedly attacked, or you are being persecuted and feel as if you're all alone?

📖 There are no easy answers, and I don't mean for anything I say to sound like a Christian cliché, but during the difficult times, *you must hold on to what you know to be true*. Read each of the following Scripture passages and write its truth in the blank.

Matthew 5:11, 12

_____

_____

_____

John 14:6

_____

_____

2 Timothy 4:17, 18

_____

_____

_____

1 Peter 1:6–9

_____

_____

_____

1 Peter 4:12–16

_____

_____

_____

These verses are meant to give encouragement, but they also point out a harsh reality—if you are a believer and follower of Jesus Christ, *you will suffer persecution*! It may not be of a physical nature, but it *will* happen.

APPLY Have you ever been persecuted for your faith? Explain.

_____

_____

_____

📖 Not only do we need to hold on to the truths of God's Word, but we need to arm and protect ourselves. The Bible says we are in a battle and

During the difficult times in your life, you must hold on to what (or who) you know to be true.

If you are a believer and follower of Jesus Christ, you will suffer persecution!

we have a real enemy: *"For our struggle is not against flesh and blood, but against the rulers, against the powers, against the world forces of this darkness, against the spiritual forces of wickedness in the heavenly places"* (Ephesians 6:12). After each verse below, describe what we can do to better prepare ourselves to serve the Lord.

Ecclesiastes 4:9–12

_____

_____

_____

Matthew 5:44

_____

_____

_____

Ephesians 6:10–18

_____

_____

_____

2 Peter 1:3–10

_____

_____

_____

The apostle Paul probably suffered more persecution than any other believer in the New Testament, but as he neared the end of his life, this is what he said: *"I have fought the good fight, I have finished the course, I have kept the faith; in the future there is laid up for me the crown of righteousness, which the Lord, the righteous Judge, will award to me on that day; and not only to me, but also to all who have loved His appearing"* (2 Timothy 4:7, 8). I pray that each of us will be able to say the same about our lives.

In the World, but Not of the World

Joseph's caravan was finally headed down a much more pleasant path—he managed the entire household of a wealthy Egyptian official who was part of Pharaoh's court. Joseph was living quite well (considering he was still a slave). He could have been taken in by the affluence and grandeur, and succumbed to the cultural and religious influences of his surroundings. He could have worshipped Potiphar's gods with the rest of the family. He could have simply used his natural skills, intelligence, and good looks to work his way to the top. He could have lived a reasonably stress-free life. After all he'd been through, he deserved a bit of the good life. Right?

He could have, but he *didn't*. If Joseph had adapted to the culture, Potiphar never would have recognized that it was the Lord working in his life, and the Lord would not have been able to use Joseph to eventually bring his family to Egypt. Jehovah would have been just another god. Joseph was *in* Egypt, but he didn't become *part of* Egypt. The very God that was contrary

"Let your light shine before men in such a way that they may see your good works, and glorify your Father who is in heaven."

Matthew 5:16

to everything Egypt stood for was the very thing that set Joseph apart from the other slaves. He could have been just another good guy, but he honored and glorified God in everything he did.

As Joseph had to live in Egypt, we have to live in this world, but we don't have to join in the sinful practices of our culture. According to Romans 12:2 we should not _____ _____ to the world, but we should _____ our _____. We need to live transformed lives that honor the Lord and show the world that Jehovah is the one true God—that Jesus is the Way, the Truth, and the Life. *"For you have been bought with a price: therefore glorify God in your body"* (1 Corinthians 6:20).

The Scripture doesn't say if there were other believers in Potiphar's household, but this is my personal opinion: If Joseph's words and conduct convinced his pagan master that the Lord was with him and was the motivation behind his good works and character, I believe he had the same influence on others in the household, and that eventually some believed in Jehovah as the one true God. When I get to heaven, and after I've met the Lord Jesus and been reunited with my loved ones, I'm going find Joseph and get the story directly from him!

Don Newman, a dear friend of mine, shared with me that each time he and his sisters walked out the door his parents gave them a precious reminder: *Remember who you are. Remember who you belong to.*

Joseph remembered he was a son of promise; he remembered he belonged to Jehovah. You, too, are a child of promise, a child of the King.

PURITY: WHAT'S THE BIG DEAL? EVERYBODY'S DOING IT

Walking by Faith—Again!

DAY THREE

Pray this verse: *"Open my eyes, that I may behold Wonderful things from Your law."* (Psalm 119:18)

If I were to ask you to name what is most important to you, I'm guessing you would say things such as the Lord, family relationships, church, home, job, and friends. This would be a list of things and people you love and cherish. They also would be of significance and value to those who love you, because what matters to you matters to them.

And so it is with purity; it's important to the Lord because He loves and cherishes us. And if we love Him, what matters to Him should matter to us. Jesus said to His disciples, *"If you love Me, you will keep My commandments"* (John 14:15) and, *"He who does not love Me does not keep My words"* (John 14:24a). If we genuinely love the Lord, we will agree with what He says in His Word and do our best to obey.

We live in a society that no longer values sexual purity. Adultery is still frowned upon to some degree, but premarital sex has become the norm and

Remember who you are. Remember who you belong to.

"And if you belong to Christ, then you are Abraham's offspring, heirs according to promise." Galatians 3:29 (NASB 1977)

is a virtual expectation in dating relationships. Even casual sex for momentary gratification is considered acceptable. Everybody's doing it—even many Christians. So, is it a big deal? Is sexual purity outdated?

📖 Read each of the following verses, and then note God's view of sexual purity.

Mark 10:6–9, 19

_____

_____

1 Corinthians 6:13–20

_____

_____

Colossians 3:1–5

_____

_____

1 Thessalonians 4:3–8

_____

_____

Hebrews 13:4

_____

_____

Pure on Purpose
📖 Read Genesis 39:6b–10.

Describe Joseph's physical appearance.

_____

_____

_____

Why did Joseph refuse Mrs. Potiphar's advances?

_____

_____

_____

Was she deterred by Joseph's refusals?

_____

_____

_____

Joseph wasn't just handsome, he had a great physique, too, and the effect was not lost on Potiphar's wife. But good looks are not always a blessing. "Apart from moral goodness and spiritual grace, physical beauty is apt to be

> **"If you love Me, you will keep My commandments."**
> **John 14:15**

> **"Joseph said, 'How then could I do this great evil and sin against God?'"**
> **Genesis 39:9b**

a fatal gift, fatal to its possessor and to whoever casts eyes upon it—a curse, not a blessing."[2] Yes, she was obviously smitten; even after he rejected her advances, she pursued him daily. But Joseph was pure on purpose; he knew that sinning against another person was a sin against God, but that to keep himself pure was to honor God. He thought purity was a big deal because God thinks it's a big deal, and Joseph loved God.

Satan would like to distract us with "Why not?" like a child asking, "Why can't I?" "What's wrong with it?" He'd like us to believe that purity is some kind of a regulation God wants to impose on us to take away pleasure. To the contrary, the sexual union between a man and a woman was created by God and is vastly important to Him. He wants us to be passionate about one another, but within the confines of marriage. If you think God is prudish about sex, read through the book of Song of Solomon (or Song of Songs) to see how much He wants us to enjoy physical intimacy.

That intimacy is a picture of the closeness God wants us to experience with Him. But like a jealous lover, He is a jealous God and wants us to worship only Him, just as we are to share our bodies with only one person in marriage. Experimenting with multiple partners is like experimenting with other gods or idols.

📖 Read Ephesians 5:25–33.

To what is a husband's love for his wife compared (v. 25)?

_____

_____

Why did Christ give Himself up (on the cross) for the church (believers) (v. 26)?

_____

_____

_____

How does Christ want to present the church to Himself (v. 27)?

_____

_____

_____

The "church" in this passage refers to those who are believers in Christ as Savior, not a specific congregation. Because He died to cleanse us of our sin, He wants us to live pure lives by figuratively washing ourselves through obedience to His Word. Marriage is a spiritual picture of Christ's love and sacrifice and His relationship with believers; it illustrates the New Covenant He fulfilled by His death, burial, and resurrection. Sexual immorality distorts that image.

📖 Read 1 Corinthians 6:19, 20.

Our bodies are the temple of the _____ _____.
To whom do our bodies belong? _____
We are to use our bodies to _____ God.

> "Our problem is not simply an epidemic of divorce; our problem is that the average American shrugs at sexual immorality, and shame has disappeared."
>
> **Jeannie St. John Taylor**

God created our sexual appetites, but that God-given appetite can only be fully satisfied with the God-given gift of marriage.

In Search of Intimacy

John 15–17 describes the oneness and intimacy between Jesus the Son, the Father, and the Holy Spirit, and how Jesus longs to share that intimacy with us. He prayed that the disciples and future believers would comprehend that relationship and glorify the Father through their lives. Can you picture Jesus praying for a spiritually close relationship with us? How then can we even think about dishonoring our bodies through sexual impurity?

Once again, Satan has lied to the world and distorted the picture of closeness God intended. He's made it into a hollow encounter between people using vain flattery to get momentary physical satisfaction. God intended for the physical relationship to be about pleasure and reproduction, the ultimate cherished union between a husband and a wife in marriage.

Lies We Believe

I don't know about you, but I hate it when someone lies to me. It shows disrespect for me and a disregard for the truth. Satan, the master liar, has sold the world a pack of lies about moral purity, and sadly, even some Christians have bought into it. He says:

- There's nothing wrong with sex between consenting partners. No one will get hurt.
- If sex produces an unwanted or inconvenient pregnancy, abort it; it's not a real baby anyway.
- You need to be sexually compatible. It's like a test drive—you keep trying till you find the right model for you.
- It's better to live together before you get married; your marriage will have a better chance of succeeding.
- Even if God disapproves of sexual immorality, it's no worse than any other sin.

Satan conveniently omits mention of the serious health risks linked to multiple sexual partners; the lifelong guilt associated with abortion and the devastation it can create for entire families; that with each new partner you're giving away a piece of your heart you will never get back; that the divorce rate among those who live together before marriage is higher than those who don't; and that the consequences of sexual immorality can be enormous.

Are you willing to exchange truth for a lie? Are you willing to exchange momentary pleasure for God's best for your life? I'm not, and neither was Joseph.

Here's the bottom line: God says sexual immorality is sin. There are no biblical loopholes. Some try to use the Bible to defend their promiscuity, but I know what God says, and I will not presume I (or anyone else) can quarrel or disagree with Him.

📖 Read Galatians 6:7 once again and fill in the blanks. *"Do not be _____, God is not _____; for whatever a man _____, this he will also _____."*

I realize many of you participating in this study have made mistakes in the past, or may be in relationships even now that are not God-honoring. If

"Whenever [Satan] speaks a lie, he speaks from his own nature, for he is a liar and the father of lies."

John 8:44b

we've learned anything in this study so far it is that God is gracious, He forgives, and He desires to use each of us for His glory no matter how much we've messed up. Don't despair, and don't beat yourself up with guilt. Here's what you can do:

- Ask God to forgive you, and then accept His forgiveness (1 John 1:9).

- Make a new start (2 Corinthians 5:17–19).

- Don't let Satan condemn you and keep throwing it in your face (Revelation 12:9,10), for Jesus is your Advocate and is defending you before the throne of the Father (1 John 2:1).

- There may be consequences you will have to deal with, but remember that you are forgiven (Romans 8:1).

- Face your future in victory (1 Corinthians 15:57, 58).

- Set new goals and boundaries; allow God to transform your life (Romans 12:1, 2).

- We are all guilty of impure thoughts and actions to one degree or another. Extend God's grace to others as He extended it to you (John 8:7).

SHE'S AFTER ME! FLEEING IMMORALITY

Walking by Faith— Again!

DAY FOUR

Pray this verse: *"Open my eyes, that I may behold Wonderful things from Your law."* (Psalm 119:18)

The story of Joseph rejecting his master's wife's advances is told in a few short verses, perhaps giving the impression it was easy for him to resist temptation. But let's review and look at it in a bit more depth. Once again, read Genesis 39:6b–10.

Give every reason you can think of why she was attracted to Joseph.

_____

_____

_____

How are her feelings for Joseph described (v. 7)?

_____

_____

_____

What reason did Joseph give for refusing her advances (v. 9)?

_____

_____

How persistent was she (v. 10)?

_____

_____

Clearly, Joseph had inherited his mother's beautiful face and form. Additionally, he was honest, diligent, intelligent, and courteous, and he managed the household well, while rising in status among the other servants. No wonder he appealed to Potiphar's wife; what was there about him not to like? It wasn't wrong for her to be attracted to Joseph—to find someone physically pleasing can't be helped—but it's what she did after the initial attraction that caused the problem. Instead of reining in her feelings, she allowed them to turn to lust, and then continued to feed her desires.

I believe that verse 10 is the key to understanding Joseph's character. He didn't just resist a few flirtatious propositions, he stood firm in the midst of intense temptation for an extended period of time, showing great strength of character. Potiphar's wife didn't make one or two passes at him, and she wasn't subtle about her intentions. The Hebrew word *yowm,* translated "day after day," implies she pursued him every day, throughout the day.

Joseph could have used any number of excuses to justify giving in to the pressure. He had been kidnapped, nearly killed, and sold into slavery. After a few years in Potiphar's household he had worked his way up the slave ladder, but he still wasn't free. He was even so conscientious his master worried about nothing regarding his house. Joseph did everything he could to honor the Lord with his life, yet from man's perspective, where did it get him?

What thoughts and emotions, possibly including doubts, do you think Joseph may have experienced while his master's wife was pursuing him?

_____

_____

_____

Can you imagine what Joseph went through each night as he lay in bed aching for his family, questioning his future, and dreading the next encounter with her? Her advances would have aroused his natural passions, because that's what attention and flattery do, and no matter who we are, our egos are fed when someone displays interest in us. But Joseph didn't allow her smooth talk to sway him. He didn't say to himself, *Perhaps just once; who would know?* Joseph realized that if he committed adultery the sin would be against God, Potiphar, his wife, and himself. Even if no else knew, God would know, and others would be hurt in the process, because sin never affects just one person. Yet Joseph was as direct in his refusals as Potiphar's wife was in her advances. He didn't go into long explanations about why adultery was wrong, he simply called it what it was—sin— and said no.

📖 Read Genesis 39:11–20.

Describe Potiphar's wife's final attempt at seducing Joseph.

_____

_____

_____

What did Joseph do?

_____

_____

_____

We don't know if the house was empty by design, or if Potiphar's wife had planned it—either way, she took advantage of the situation. Until this time, Joseph had done all he could to ward off her advances. He told her no, called it sin, invoked the name of his God, and avoided contact when he could. But this time she didn't try verbal seduction; she went for the physical approach and grabbed Joseph's clothing. Put yourself in Joseph's place; once again, he was in a seemingly no-win situation. If he continued to refuse the advances of his master's wife, he risked her anger and possible punishment. If he gave in to sin, he would be forsaking his God, betraying his master, defrauding his wife, and destroying his own testimony. But Joseph didn't pause to consider his options—*he simply ran*. He chose to do right even when no one was looking; he chose to take a stand no matter what the cost.

Sometimes the Bad Guy Wins—but Not Forever!

Do you ever feel as if the bad guys always win? We know they don't, but sometimes it seems that way. Potiphar's wife, the scorned and rejected woman, plotted, lied, accused, and contrived evidence to incriminate Joseph. She even cast blame on her husband for employing him. Joseph did everything right: He remained faithful to the Lord, honored his master, resisted the woman's advances, and then fled when she physically assailed him. And where did it get him? Prison!

Perhaps you're in a situation now where you are doing everything right, but the "bad guys" seem to be winning, and you feel as if you're on your way to a prison of sorts. Remember three things:

- The Lord is with you, as He was with Joseph (Genesis 39:2, 21, 23).
- Everyone will answer for their actions (Romans 14:10–12).
- Don't fret—God will take care of the wicked (Psalm 37).

 Describe a time when you did what was right and it appeared the bad guy won. How did the Lord resolve the issue?

_____

_____

_____

_____

When in Doubt—Run!

Temptation does not always come in the form of blatant evil; if it did, it would be much easier to recognize and resist. I've noticed temptation often comes during times of success and prosperity, as it did in Joseph's case. Those are the times we let down our guard because we think we have it all together. That's why it's vital we keep the armor of God on at all times and cover ourselves in prayer (Ephesians 6:10–18).

As you've participated in today's lesson, I'm confident you have noted similarities between your life and Joseph's. Perhaps your temptation is not moral impurity, but of another nature. It makes no difference, because we all struggle with the lure of sin, and the answers are the same.

Let's look at some practical advice from God's Word. Write the biblical counsel found in each verse.

> **"The eyes of the LORD are in every place, Watching the evil and the good."**
> **Proverbs 15:3**

> **Joseph chose to do right even when no one was looking; he chose to take a stand no matter what the cost.**

Psalm 1:1–3

_____

_____

Proverbs 1:10

_____

_____

1 Corinthians 6:18

_____

_____

When faced with a sinful choice, Joseph ran. What do you do?

1 Corinthians 10:12–14

_____

_____

2 Corinthians 10:5

_____

_____

Galatians 5:16

_____

_____

2 Timothy 2:22

_____

_____

No matter what your temptation, the Scriptures are clear: Be choosy in your friendships; when sinners lure you, get away from them; don't assume you can't be tempted; guard your thoughts; walk in the Spirit; flee youthful lusts. Joseph's position as a slave made his situation somewhat unique. He couldn't find employment elsewhere. There was no place for him to flee temptation except to another part of the house. He couldn't completely avoid Potiphar's wife; he could only try to evade her or have others present. At last, he did the only thing possible, which was to run.

📖 Read Hebrews 2:17, 18. How do we know that Christ understands our temptations?

_____

_____

_____

Jesus Christ knows our temptations because he was tempted in every area in which we've been tempted. _Every_ area! He will give us a way to escape, but we must take it at the first opportunity, as Joseph did. Do not fool around with sin, and do not expect to see a door of escape if you keep closing it!

I don't know what your temptation is, or the circumstances, but you may need to just get out. It may mean finding another job, joining a different gym, attending another church, or making new friendships. But, **you must flee!** Don't assume you can handle it, and don't think you can flirt with temptation without being burned, for *"When lust has conceived, it gives birth to sin; and when sin is accomplished, it brings forth death. Do not be deceived, my beloved brethren"* (James 1:15, 16) Emphasis mine.

As we close today's lesson, I want to give you some final thoughts. First, remember that Jesus understands your temptation, and that He wants to deliver you. But, you must guard your heart and mind through prayer and spending time in the Scriptures. For some people, like Potiphar's wife, sin is a game. They want what they can't have, and pursue it at all costs, indifferent to who they hurt in the process. Don't be beguiled by flattery and don't try to handle situations like this on your own—find an accountability partner in whom you can trust and confide. Don't think you can toy with sin and get away with it. When rejecting ungodliness, remember Joseph. He was direct, but courteous; he wasn't afraid to call sin evil; he acknowledged the Lord; and he ran!

And finally, fleeing evil will not always entail running physically—it also can be emotional or spiritual. You must guard your emotions, and you must be careful you are not swayed by unsound biblical teachings. *"We are no longer to be children, tossed here and there by waves and carried about by every wind of doctrine, by the trickery of men, by craftiness in deceitful scheming"* (Ephesians 4:14).

 Have you experienced physical/sensual temptation at work? Somewhere else? How did you deal with it? Or how *are* you dealing with it?

_____

_____

_____

_____

FOR ME TO FOLLOW GOD

Walking by Faith—Again!

DAY FIVE

Pray this verse: *"Open my eyes, that I may behold Wonderful things from Your law."* (Psalm 119:18)

After a few years in Potiphar's household, things were starting to look up for Joseph—God was with him; his master's home and properties were being blessed because of him; and the Lord honored him in all he did. He really had turned his job into a ministry.

But it couldn't have been easy for Joseph to follow God. As strong as Joseph was, even he must have struggled with loneliness, discouragement, and hopelessness. If you look at his life without God in the picture, he should have given up. But God *was* in the picture, and He is in yours, too. He is weaving each thread of the tapestry of your life to make a master-

God is the Artist transforming you into a masterpiece, and He is an Artist worth following.

piece. You may not feel like a work of art, but if there's one thing I've learned as I've visited historic homes and museums—the beauty of artwork is in the eye of the beholder, and our heavenly Father is "beholding" you! He is the Artist who is transforming you into a masterpiece, and He is an Artist worth following.

To what does Isaiah 64:8 compare us?

_____

_____

_____

What does a potter do with clay?

_____

_____

_____

If a piece of clay on the potter's wheel doesn't initially take the right shape, it's broken down to be re-formed—sometimes several times. That's what God is doing with us. He's shaping us and molding us into vessels for His glory, but that process can be agonizing. God was breaking down Joseph again and again, molding him into a work of art, and the process was painful. Yet, in the end, it was worth it, just as it will be for you and me. *"Beloved, now we are children of God, and it has not appeared as yet what we will be. We know that when He appears, we will be like Him, because we will see Him just as He is. And everyone who has this hope fixed on Him purifies himself, just as He is pure"* (1 John 3:2, 3).

APPLY How do you see that God has been molding your life through your work, home, church, or other situation?

_____

_____

_____

The Lord was with Joseph, but Joseph was also with the Lord.

It is stated three times in Genesis 39 that *the "LORD" (Jehovah) was with Joseph*. Why do you think God stressed that point?

_____

_____

_____

I think the Lord wanted future believers to know He is with them even when they feel as if they're alone—no matter what the circumstances. Joseph didn't have anyone reading Scriptures or praying with him during this difficult time. He only could hang on to what he knew about the Lord—that He is faithful; that He has a purpose and a plan; and that He was Joseph's Protector, his Deliverer, his Shield, and his Hope.

📖 Let's look at another man who put his hope in the Lord during a difficult time. Read 1 Samuel 30:1–6.

What did David's men want to do to him when they discovered the women and children were gone?

_____

_____

_____

What did David do?

_____

_____

_____

In their grief, David's men wanted to stone him, but verse 6 says, *"David strengthened himself in the LORD his God."* The Hebrew word translated "strengthen" (*chazaq*) means "to fasten upon, seize, be courageous." When David was all alone and everyone was against him, he fastened himself upon the Lord and there found his strength and courage. Sometimes it will be that way for you, too. You may feel as if everyone and everything is against you, but like David, you must fasten yourself to the promises of God.

According to 2 Peter 1:3, where do we get everything we need pertaining to life and godliness?

_____

_____

_____

What seven character qualities are we to diligently add to our faith (vv. 5–7)?

_____

_____

_____

Joseph's strength, courage, self-control, and godliness didn't just happen; he diligently applied these things to his faith and continued to walk with God on a daily basis. King David had severe moral failings, because he let down his guard (2 Samuel 11). Instead of going out to battle as he should have, he stayed home, saw Bathsheba bathing on her rooftop, committed adultery, and had her husband killed. When David was tempted, he did not flee. When Joseph's brother Reuben was tempted to sleep with Jacob's concubine Bilhah, he did not flee (Genesis 35:22). When Judah was tempted to hire Tamar posing as a harlot, he did not flee (Genesis 38). In sharp contrast to Joseph's dealings with Potiphar's wife, each of these men *pursued* immorality—Joseph ran from it.

When David saw Bathsheba bathing he should have fled from temptation at that very moment. Instead, he inquired about her, and then sent his attendants to bring her to his home. God did not deliver David from temptation because he wasn't where he was supposed to be, or doing what he was supposed to be doing—he was toying with sin. But, God did deliver Joseph, because he was where he was supposed to be, he was doing what he was supposed to be doing, and he fled from temptation. God will provide a way of escape, but you can't dabble with sin and go unscathed.

The manner of God's deliverance may not come packaged the way we want it. When God delivered Joseph from death and the pit, it was into the hands

> **"No temptation has overtaken you but such as is common to man; and God is faithful, who will not allow you to be tempted beyond what you are able, but with the temptation will provide the way of escape also, so that you will be able to endure it."**
>
> **1 Corinthians 10:13**

Sometimes following God means we must advance into the unknown.

of slave traders. When He delivered him from Mrs. Potiphar, it was into prison. Most of us would not consider either of those solutions to be deliverance, but—God knew the end of Joseph's story, and He knows the end of yours! Sometimes following God means we must advance into the unknown.

What attracted David to Bathsheba (2 Samuel 11:2)?

_____

_____

What attracted Potiphar's wife to Joseph (Genesis 39:6)?

_____

_____

Many cultures, including ours, place an inordinate importance on youth and beauty, as was the case with both King David and Potiphar's wife. God is the original designer of beauty, and He created us to be drawn to it, but we have a responsibility to regard it with deference. Likewise, those with unusual beauty have a duty to refrain from using their looks to defraud or tempt anyone who is not their spouse. Our clothing, too, should be modest (1 Timothy 2:9). In other words, it's morally wrong to knowingly dress so as to unduly entice the opposite sex (that goes for women *and* men). As speaker/author Beth Moore says, "We dress on purpose."

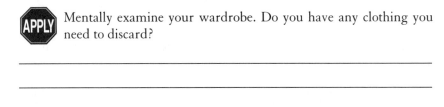 Mentally examine your wardrobe. Do you have any clothing you need to discard?

_____

_____

_____

It is morally wrong to knowingly dress so as to unduly entice the opposite sex (that goes for women and men).

Whether or not Bathsheba was a willing partner, David abused his power as king in summoning her to the palace. The wife of Potiphar, too, abused her authority as mistress of her house in pursuing Joseph. As a leader, boss, manager, or other person of influence, you must never use your authority to solicit immoral conduct. And, as a person under authority, you should never submit to anyone taking advantage of his or her power to try to coerce you to do anything contrary to God's Word.

I know this week's lessons have been difficult for some of you to complete because they've brought up memories of the distant past, or perhaps the not-so-distant past. I want to leave you with encouragement as you follow God.

- We are *all* guilty of moral failures. *"As it is written, 'THERE IS NONE RIGHTEOUS, NOT EVEN ONE'"* (Romans 3:10).

- *"There is therefore now no condemnation for those who are in Christ Jesus"* (Romans 8:1).

- When King David confessed his sin he was cleansed and restored to fellowship with the Lord (Psalm 51).

- Judah was blessed by Jacob to be in the lineage of Jesus *after* he slept with Tamar.

- If God only used people who were always morally upstanding, He couldn't use anyone—even Joseph was not perfect.

Precious Heavenly Father, Thank You for my job, at home, outside the home, or in the church. Help me see it as a ministry and to serve those with whom I work. Thank You for being with me during the times I feel alone, even when I don't sense Your presence. Help me to remember You are always near. Thank You for new beginnings. I purpose in my heart to keep myself morally pure, and when I do sin, I will come to You for forgiveness. Thank You for providing a way for me to escape temptation, and help me not to toy with sin. In Jesus' name, amen.

Works Cited

1. Theodore H. Epp, *Joseph: God Planned It for Good* (Lincoln, NE: Back to the Bible, 1982), 55.

2. Joseph Strahan, *Hebrew Ideals* (Grand Rapids, MI: Kregel Publications, 1982), 289.

Notes

6

Life at the Top

I love the thrill of a roller coaster—that slow climb to the first peak, the anticipation of the rapid descent on the other side, the unknown of the next turn. By the time I reach the end of the ride, I'm usually ready to go again. But when the events of my life are up and down, and I don't know what the next curve or plunge will bring, it's not so thrilling.

At this point in our study, Joseph's life was definitely a roller coaster. He probably thought the dips and turns had just become comfortably predictable when his roller coaster seemed to plummet into an abyss. But Joseph's ride was far from over.

Perhaps you feel like a roller coaster aptly represents your life, and you're fearful of the next dip or turn. Hang on, and remember—you're not alone. Now, let's join Joseph as he continues the ride of his life.

LIFE WAS SO MUCH BETTER IN THE PAST

Pray this verse: *"Open my eyes, that I may behold Wonderful things from Your law."* (Psalm 119:18)

When going through particularly difficult circumstances, our tendency is to either wish for things to be as they were in the past, or long for a trouble-free future. The difficulty with either prospect is that people become so focused on what was, or what is to come, they neglect to make the most of the here and now.

Those living in the past tend to talk about how much better things were in the "good old days." Perhaps, but memories can become romanticized and people forget there are trials in every era. Others live in a past filled with regrets. They think about what they should or shouldn't have done, sometimes carrying loads of guilt, or hang on to real or perceived offenses, existing as a victim. And then there are those who live in past glories. They haven't done anything worthwhile in years, so they feel compelled to remind everyone of their long-ago accomplishments.

Consider Joseph's life before he was thrown into prison. List some events in his life that could have induced him to live in the past.

_____

_____

_____

> **"I shall remember the deeds of the LORD; Surely I will remember Your wonders of old. I will meditate on all Your work And muse on Your deeds."**
>
> **Psalm 77:11, 12**

Joseph certainly could have lived in regret over what might have been. He could have complained about the wrongs done to him by his family, fretted over his lost wealth and position, and been bitter over the betrayal by his master's wife. He could have been a "drama king" and complained how he did everything right, but God let everything go wrong. Joseph was only human, and certainly thoughts such as these passed through his mind, but evidently he didn't allow them to linger.

I don't mean to imply there is no place for recalling, and even enjoying, the past; after all, God is the One who created our minds with the capacity to remember. In fact, I can think of three good reasons to remember past events. One is for the pure joy of good memories; two is so we won't repeat the same mistakes; and three is what I believe kept Joseph going through the rough times. I'll explain, but first, please read Psalm 77:1–13.

Some years ago, my husband and I were facing the devastating prospect of losing $7,000, which we could ill afford to lose. One afternoon as I was fretting (and praying), I picked up my Bible to seek direction and hope. It literally fell open to Psalm 77. Though I had read this chapter countless times, and even had it underlined, it was like seeing it for the first time.

The first six verses perfectly described my frustrations. I cried to the Lord; I couldn't sleep; I couldn't think about anything except that $7,000. Then I read verses 7 through 9. I picked up my pen and wrote "No!" after each of the six questions. *"Will the Lord reject forever?"* No! *"And will He never be favorable again?"* No! *"Has His lovingkindness ceased forever?"* No! *"Has His promise come to an end forever?"* No! *"Has God forgotten to be gracious?"* No! *"Or has He in anger withdrawn His compassion?"* No! I then read verses 10 through 13. Even in the psalmist's despair he chose to *remember* the works, wonders, and deeds the Lord had done *in the past*. Remembering how the Lord had got him through trials gave him confidence He would do it again! I began to make a list of the times the Lord had seen us through other hardships and had miraculously provided our needs. The problem was resolved later, but in the meantime, I knew He would see us through as He had so many times.

Previously in our study, we saw how family history and God's statutes and promises were passed down by word of mouth from generation to generation, for they didn't yet have the written Word of God. Joseph knew those stories well. Don't you think he was encouraged during his trials as he remembered God's wondrous works of the past? For if God could deliver Noah, He could deliver Joseph. If God could provide a sacrificial ram for Isaac, He could provide for Joseph. If God could rescue Joseph from death in a desert pit, He could rescue him from an Egyptian prison. Yes, God wants us to remember the glories of the past—but, *His* glories, not ours. He wants us to boast about the past—*His* past, not ours.

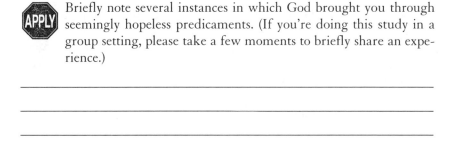 Briefly note several instances in which God brought you through seemingly hopeless predicaments. (If you're doing this study in a group setting, please take a few moments to briefly share an experience.)

_____

_____

_____

_____

When we share what God's done in our lives, it gives hope and encouragement to others. It tells them He is faithful, He still performs miracles, and He still meets needs. I wonder if we have been remiss in not passing down the wonders of God's faithfulness to the next generation.

Living in the future can be just as futile as living in the past. I'll admit I struggle with this much more than looking to past regrets. I tend to grit my teeth, and say, "This too shall pass," then try to endure the trial as best I can. Fortunately, most difficulties pass with time, but if we just try to tolerate the problem 'til it's over, we miss the blessing of the trial. Yes, you read correctly—*there are blessings in trials*.

What are the benefits of trials and affliction found in each of the following passages?

Psalm 119:67

_____

_____

Don't lose the blessing of the past in the pain of the present.

Trials will make us bitter or better—Joseph chose "better."

Psalm 119:71

_____

_____

Psalm 119:75

_____

_____

Romans 5:1–5

_____

_____

James 1:2–4

_____

_____

1 Peter 4:12–14

_____

_____

The wonder of Joseph's story is not that he endured his trials, but the manner in which he endured them. He served, honored, and glorified God in the midst of them. Certainly, he reflected on the past and wondered what would happen in the future, that was clear by the names he gave his sons, but he always made the most of the present.

Live in the present with an eternal perspective. Learn from the past, live in the present, hope in the future. Savor every moment. Create good memories.

📖 According to the following verses, why does God stress the importance of living in the present?

Proverbs 27:1

_____

_____

Matthew 6:25–34

_____

_____

James 4:13–17

_____

_____

Having a biblical view of the future is just as important as having a godly perspective of the past. One day I was talking to my son David on the phone—okay, I was whining about my circumstances. After listening for a few minutes, he said, "Mom, it's going to get better; it just may not be until you get to heaven." I didn't want to hear that, but he was right! We are going to have trials and struggles here on Earth, but that which is waiting for us in heaven will make it all worthwhile. We may not realize our rewards on Earth, but the rewards God has for us in eternity will be more than we can imagine.

📖 Read Hebrews 11:8–16. Abraham, Isaac, Jacob, and the twelve brothers died before the children of Israel realized the fulfillment of the Abrahamic covenant, including the Promised Land. What did these patriarchs desire even more than a piece of earthly ground (v. 16)?

_____

_____

_____

📖 According to the following verses, what do we have to look forward to that makes living now worthwhile?

John 14:1–3

_____

_____

Romans 8:18

_____

_____

1 Corinthians 2:9, 10

_____

_____

1 Corinthians 3:8–15

_____

_____

2 Corinthians 5:9, 10

_____

_____

1 Peter 1:4

_____

_____

> **Our time on Earth is simply preparation for the wonders and rewards God has for us in eternity.**

> **Jesus said, "Behold, I am coming quickly, and My reward is with Me, to render to every man according to what he has done."**
>
> **(Revelation 22:12)**

We can find joy and contentment in our present circumstances not only because we know of God's past faithfulness, but because we know of His future promises. Like Joseph, we don't know what our future holds, but we do know the One who holds our future.

DOES ANYONE OUT THERE LOVE ME? FORGOTTEN—AGAIN

Life at the Top

DAY TWO

Pray this verse: *"Open my eyes, that I may behold Wonderful things from Your law."* (Psalm 119:18)

I don't think there's anything more frustrating than doing the right thing, then having it misrepresented or misunderstood. Joseph tried so hard to *not* sin with his master's wife, yet ended up wrongly accused and having to carry the stigma of sexual assault. Apparently, Joseph turned the other cheek, for there's not even a hint he tried to defend himself or expose his master's wife for who she really was. And, to make matters worse, it seems no one came to Joseph's defense, even though it's likely the other servants were aware of her ongoing sensual advances.

Read Genesis 39:19, 20. Potiphar listened to his wife's story, and he was furious, but was his anger directed at Joseph? Many scholars think he did not believe his wife's accusations, and his outrage was directed at her. In verse 14, she had insulted her husband in front of the other slaves and implied that Joseph's alleged attack against her was an affront to them as well. No wonder no one came to his defense; no wonder his master was so angry.

Potiphar had observed Joseph's upright character for several years, and he may well have known of his wife's lack of moral fiber. Yet, he could hardly side with a slave against his wife, so his options were limited. He could have had Joseph put to death—the customary sentence for attempted rape, but instead, he placed him in the prison where court officials were confined—the very prison over which he had control (compare Genesis 39:1 and Genesis 40:3). This prison was probably not as wretched as the ones reserved for common criminals, but Joseph was confined, nonetheless, and certainly didn't have the limited pleasures he had enjoyed as overseer.

Why, Lord?
Have you ever asked the Lord, "Why?" (Perhaps the better question is how many times have you asked Him, "Why?") If you have, you're in good company. Moses, David, Job, Isaiah, Jeremiah, and the disciples all asked the Lord, "Why?" at one time or another, and I'm pretty sure this was a "Why?" moment for Joseph. From a human perspective, he had done everything right—again—and everything had gone wrong—again. It *appeared* his brothers had been successful in their efforts to be rid of him. It *appeared* that Mrs. Potiphar had triumphed in her bogus allegations. But, we know better and that appearances can be deceiving.

Do you think it's wrong to ask God, "Why?" Explain your answer.

_____
_____
_____
_____

I don't think it's wrong to ask, "Why?" when we ask the question in faith. In other words, if and when the Lord chooses to answer our "whys" and clarify reasons for events or circumstances, that's fine. But, when He doesn't choose to give an explanation, we must walk in faith, and trust He has a greater purpose than what we can see or comprehend.

Please turn in your Bible to Romans 8:28 and fill in the blanks. *"And we _____ that God causes _____ things to work _____ for _____ to those who _____ God, to those who are called according to His _____."* This verse is most often quoted by

Oh, that we would live lives of such integrity that people would not believe a false accusation against us!

Christians when they are going through difficult circumstances, and it certainly has brought comfort to me on numerous occasions. Although it was written hundreds of years after Joseph's time, I believe he understood the truth that his trials were for a purpose, even though he did not understand. Why do I believe that? Compare Joseph's words in Genesis 50:19, 20 with Romans 8:28. It is virtually a mirror image of the truth the apostle Paul wrote in Romans.

Have you ever been falsely accused? Betrayed? Did anyone come to your defense? Have you been passed over for a promotion after it was promised or implied? Are you trapped in circumstances that feel like a prison to you? Are you asking God, "Why?" You're probably tired of me saying this, but it won't be the last time—*God knows the end of your story just as He knew the end of Joseph's story*. He has a purpose for your life that may not be clear at this time, but if you truly love Him, He is working *all* things together for your good and His glory!

What similarities do you see between Joseph's position in Potiphar's home and his position in prison?

_____

_____

_____

Could it be that Paul read Joseph's words himself while he was going through trials and tribulations of his own?

Try to grasp the essence of this account as if you're reading or hearing it for the first time. Think about this: *An inmate was running the prison!* Not just any inmate, and not just any prison—a young, *Hebrew slave* was managing the royal prison. Can there be any doubt God was with Joseph?

This brings us to a pivotal juncture in our study. Some of you are saying, "Bring on the trials; if Joseph can do it, I can do it." Others are saying, "Forget it—I will never be as good as Joseph, so I might as well give up now." If we compare ourselves with Joseph, we'll probably all come up lacking. Let's be clear. First, the Bible says we should not compare among ourselves (2 Corinthians 10:12).

Secondly, although Joseph was an incredible young man, he had many faults. God used the time in Potiphar's home and in prison to mature Joseph, develop his character, and teach him leadership skills. Joseph, at seventeen years of age, was not ready for God's ultimate purpose for him. He had moments of despondency just like you and me. (Remember the meaning of the names of his sons?) Later in our study we'll see several times he broke down and wept, and I imagine there were a few other tears shed during his years as a slave and a prisoner. So, don't despair. Enjoy our study, learn what you can from Joseph's life, and commit your life to honoring the Lord.

APPLY At this point in our study, what personal practical applications have you learned?

_____

_____

_____

_____

_____

Thinking of Others Instead of Yourself

📖 Read Genesis 40:1–23.

Why were the cupbearer and baker in prison (vv. 1–3)?

_____

_____

What did Joseph observe about the prisoners (vv. 6, 7)?

_____

_____

Whom did Joseph credit with the interpretation of dreams (v. 8)?

_____

_____

Joseph interpreted a dream for each man. Which man would return to his position in Pharaoh's court?

_____

_____

Which man would be executed?

_____

_____

What did Joseph ask of the cupbearer (vv. 14, 15)?

_____

_____

What did the cupbearer do when he was restored to his position (v. 23)?

_____

_____

This short passage of Scripture holds a wealth of truth. I want to share with you what I learned from Joseph's tenure in prison.

1. No job is too lowly; serve others with your whole heart, as if you were serving the Lord Himself.

2. Be observant. Notice the countenance of those around you, and your own hardships and pain will seem less important.

3. Look to the needs and welfare of others and seek to lighten their load.

4. You can change the attitudes of others (as well as the atmosphere of your surroundings) by serving them and looking out for their needs.

5. Don't be afraid to acknowledge the Lord in front of others.

6. Never take credit for the work God does through you.

7. Never be afraid to speak the truth.

8. When stating your case, don't blame others.

9. Make the most of every encounter; you never know if the person you meet in "prison" is part of God's bigger purpose for your life.

10. Keep your promises.

I know an elderly man who is a lot like Joseph. Jack is losing his eyesight and makes frequent trips to the hospital. Before he goes on each visit, he sends out an e-mail requesting prayer that God will use him to encourage the doctors, nurses, and other patients, and that he will have opportunities to share Christ with unbelievers. (And sometimes, he even asks for prayer for his own needs). Oh, that we would be like Joseph and Jack, thinking of others more than ourselves and helping to bear their burdens!

"Do nothing from selfishness or empty conceit, but with humility of mind regard one another as more important than himself; do not merely look out for your own personal interests, but also for the interests of others" (Philippians 2:3, 4).

READY OR NOT, HERE YOU GO!

Pray this verse: *"Open my eyes, that I may behold Wonderful things from Your law."* (Psalm 119:18)

At the end of yesterday's lesson we left Joseph sitting on the edge of his prison cot waiting to hear from Pharaoh's cupbearer. How long the baker and cupbearer were in prison is unknown, but Genesis 40:4 says it was for *"some time,"* and Joseph likely got to know them fairly well during that period. After serving them daily, and giving the cupbearer a favorable interpretation of his dreams, you might even say Pharaoh's servant "owed him." Joseph must have waited in eager anticipation, hoping every day that the cupbearer would remember and a court representative would come to listen to his appeal. He was twenty-eight years old and had been a slave and a prisoner for eleven years. He finally saw a possibility for deliverance, but his hopes were dashed as he was forgotten—again.

Think of the last time someone said they'd do something for you, but didn't followed through on their word. Did you run out to check the mail; reach for the phone each time it rang; rush to the door when you heard a knock? Did your stomach churn as you waited in expectation? Briefly describe the circumstances and your emotions.

_____

_____

_____

Most of the time, our lives and freedom will not be at stake as Joseph's were, but when someone has given their word and then forgotten you, it is especially hurtful.

📖 Read Proverbs 3:27, 28 and write it in your own words.

_____

_____

_____

_____

When you think you've been forgotten, remember— God is still working.

What does James 5:12 say about keeping your word?

_____

_____

📖 Read Genesis 41:1–13.

How much time had elapsed since the cupbearer was released from prison (v. 1)?

_____

_____

How many dreams did Pharaoh have?

_____

_____

The first dream involved _____ (v. 2). The second dream involved _____ _____ (v. 5).

What was Pharaoh's reaction to his dreams (v. 8)?

_____

_____

_____

Whom did Pharaoh ask to interpret his dreams (v. 8)?

_____

_____

After Pharaoh's two dreams, he called upon his magicians and wise men to discover their meaning. When they could not give him an answer, the cupbearer finally remembered Joseph and recounted to Pharaoh how his own disturbing dream had been interpreted by the Hebrew slave.

📖 Read Genesis 41:14–32.

What did Pharaoh do when the cupbearer told him about Joseph's ability to interpret dreams (v. 14)?

_____

_____

How did Joseph prepare himself to go before Pharaoh?

_____

_____

_____

Pharaoh's dreams had continued to disturb him, and he was desperate to know their meaning—so desperate, he was willing to seek help from a prisoner—*a Hebrew prisoner!* As for Joseph, he had been waiting for two long years for some word from the palace about a possible release. Suddenly, officials rushed into the prison, told him to bathe, shave, and change his clothes to prepare to meet the leader of one of the most powerful nations in the world. No doubt he had often rehearsed his defense, but he never expected this.

Can you imagine the thoughts going through Joseph's mind—his heart racing as he made himself presentable for Pharaoh? Perhaps he was praying, asking the Lord for courage, wisdom, and clarity of speech. Whatever his thoughts may have been, Joseph was ready: ready to stand before a pagan king who believed himself to be a god; ready to declare that his God was the true God, the all-knowing God, the God of dreams, and the God of answers.

Are you ready? Are you prepared to speak for the Lord at every opportunity? Has He been preparing you for a special task? You may not be called upon to be in the public eye or do things that will bring great acclaim, but are you ready for the unexpected? Preparing to meet Pharaoh had little to do with physical preparation; it had everything to do with honoring his Lord by being a model slave and an honest overseer, saying no to seduction, and looking out for the needs of others even when it appeared no one was looking out for him. God used those thirteen years to get Joseph ready—developing his leadership skills, his humility, and his dependence upon God. Joseph spent those thirteen years meeting every trial head-on and being obedient.

What do the following verses say about being ready to speak for the Lord?

Colossians 4:6

_____

_____

1 Peter 3:15

_____

_____

APPLY Do you spend time wishing and hoping and thinking about what you want for your future, but neglect to live in the moment? _____

Do you want the end result without having to go through the "getting ready" process? _____

Are you ready for God's unexpected in your life? _____

In Genesis 41:15 there are seven words that I believe speak a multitude about Joseph's character: *"I have heard it said about you . . ."* Joseph's reputation preceded him. He was only a Hebrew slave and prisoner, but he conducted himself in such a way no one had anything negative to say about him.

APPLY How about you? What would a person say upon meeting you for the first time? "I've heard it said about your:

Speech . . .

_____

_____

_____

Did You Know?
EGYPTIAN CULTURE

The Egyptians shaved their entire bodies and were fastidiously clean, sometimes bathing more than once a day. Men and women alike wore wigs and makeup.

Be ready while God is getting you ready.

Temper . . .

_____

_____

_____

Business dealings . . .

_____

_____

_____

Integrity (or lack thereof) . . .

_____

_____

_____

Moral conduct . . .

_____

_____

_____

Marriage . . .

_____

_____

_____

Church . . .

_____

_____

_____

Other . . .

_____

_____

_____

What answer did Joseph give when Pharaoh asked him about interpreting dreams?

_____

_____

_____

Joseph knew he couldn't give the interpretation, but he knew God could. His answer was not a noble effort at false humility; Joseph really knew he could do nothing without the Lord. That reality is stated again in John

15:1–5 when Jesus tells His disciples, *"Apart from Me you can do nothing"* (v. 5b). Pharaoh had sought the wisdom of his magicians and skilled men, but they could not give him an answer. So God chose a lowly slave through whom to display His might and wisdom.

Read 1 Corinthians 1:18–31.

What has God done with the wisdom of the world (v. 20)?

_____

_____

_____

What is wiser than men (v. 25)?

_____

_____

_____

What is stronger than men (v. 25)?

_____

_____

_____

God has chosen the _____ _____, _____
_____, _____ _____, and the _____
_____ _____ ____ (vv. 27, 28).

Four times (Genesis 41:16, 25, 28, 32) Joseph invoked the Lord as he interpreted Pharaoh's dreams, and that was no small matter. It wasn't like some sports personality saying, "Praise the Lord!" after a game. It was a young Hebrew prisoner telling the "supreme god of Egypt" that his God was the only true and supreme God, the Creator, the King, the Judge, and the Savior. For two years Joseph had hoped for an opportunity to present his case of innocence before Pharaoh, and here was his chance. He could have flattered Pharaoh with accolades, but he honored the Lord instead. He could have bargained or asked for a special favor, but always thinking of others, Joseph came with a servant's heart and kept the focus on the matter troubling the king. He didn't try to show up the magicians; he didn't try to manipulate the circumstances; he just . . . served.

In Genesis 41:25–32, Joseph gives Pharaoh the interpretation of his dreams. What did the seven fat cows and the seven good ears of grain represent?

_____

_____

What did the seven lean cows and the seven thin ears of grain represent?

_____

_____

_____

> **"Not to us, O LORD, not to us, But to Your name give glory."**
>
> **Psalm 115:1a**

Why did Pharaoh have two dreams (v. 32)?

_____

_____

_____

Earlier, we saw in Romans 12:1, 2 how God wants us to be transformed to His will, not conformed to the world. The Greek word translated "transformed" (*metamorphoo*) means "to metamorphose," as a caterpillar transforms into a butterfly. In other words, it's a process. The word is used again in 2 Corinthians 3:18: *"And we, who with unveiled faces all reflect the Lord's glory, are being transformed into his likeness with ever-increasing glory, which comes from the Lord, who is the Spirit"* (NIV). Just as Moses' face shone with the glory of the Lord after being in His presence (2 Corinthians 3:7), so our lives should reflect His glory.

Transformation doesn't happen all at once; it's a process that continues throughout our lives. Sometimes the process is painful and difficult, but when the world sees us react to our difficulties in faith and obedience, they see us as reflecting the glory of the Lord. Joseph's process was long and sometimes agonizing, but throughout the process, others saw Jehovah in his life. His brothers saw it and wanted to kill him. Potiphar and the jailer saw it and made him an overseer. And then—Pharaoh saw it!

THE RIDE TO THE TOP

Pray this verse: *"Open my eyes, that I may behold Wonderful things from Your law."* (Psalm 119:18)

Have you ever been told you have a serious problem and then been left without a solution? It leaves you feeling helpless and frustrated. It's like a doctor diagnosing cancer in you, then walking out the door without giving you treatment. Joseph basically told Pharaoh he had cancer, but he didn't walk away without giving him a solution.

Egypt was a land of frequent flooding—the Nile flooded virtually every year. The floods left silt that created rich soil; however, if the floodwaters were low, a famine would sometimes follow. A famine of seven years would be devastating to Egypt.

📖 Read Genesis 41:33–36 and briefly describe Joseph's advice to Pharaoh.

_____

_____

_____

Joseph's counsel from the Lord to Pharaoh was brilliant. He could have just told him to find a wise man to plan for the famine (anyone would say that), but he went on to lay out an entire strategy for the disaster to come.

According to Genesis 41:37–40, how did Pharaoh and his servants respond to Joseph's advice?

_____

_____

_____

What did Pharaoh recognize in Joseph (v. 38)?

_____

_____

Joseph's story is filled with "Wow!" moments, and this is one of them. The events move so quickly it appears Joseph interpreted the dreams, presented the solution, and was appointed vizier of Egypt. However, I believe there is a break between verses 38 and 39, allowing time for Pharaoh, as a wise leader, to consult with his advisers. The person he would choose to manage Egypt during the years of plenty and the subsequent famine was of utmost importance, for the country would not get a second chance; if the man failed, the nation would starve. Egypt's reputation was at stake—and Pharaoh *was* Egypt. To entrust its future to a virtual unknown would not have been done without the careful guidance and deliberation of many men.

I think it's very possible Potiphar and the jailer were two of the men with whom Pharaoh consulted, for they knew the kind of man Joseph was. His testimony of obedience, service, and integrity had literally caught up with him. He was finally being recognized and rewarded for the man he had become through thirteen years of betrayal, rejection, and emotional pain. Joseph had every reason from a human perspective to become bitter and resentful and to act out those emotions. But if he had done so, he never would have been appointed to the position God intended him to have.

What character qualities do you think Pharaoh and his servants saw in Joseph that convinced them his interpretation of the dreams was accurate and his advice wise?

_____

_____

_____

Joseph exhibited *deference* when he physically prepared himself in the manner of Egyptians to go before Pharaoh; he showed *confidence* when he spoke without hesitation; he acted in *humility* when he gave credit to the Lord for the interpretation; he displayed *courage* by speaking of his one God before a throne-roomful of polytheists; and, he showed *respect* in the manner in which he addressed Pharaoh. Yes, Joseph's character was shining through his life.

📖 Read Matthew 5:14–16.

Who is the light of the world?

_____

_____

Jesus says *we* are the light of the world, and we should conduct ourselves in such a way people will exalt, honor, esteem, and magnify God the Father. Can you grasp the reverse meaning of that statement? People will be irreverent, dishonoring, and disrespectful toward the Lord when our conduct is unbecoming. We are God's representatives on Earth, and the world forms its view of Him based on our behavior. That is an awesome responsibility for believers, one we need to take very seriously.

APPLY How does your conduct glorify the Lord?

_____

_____

_____

What areas of your behavior need work?

_____

_____

_____

In a study on a major biblical figure such as Joseph, individuals like Pharaoh garner little attention. But I think Pharaoh exhibited some positive leadership skills from which we can learn:

1. He punished swiftly (the baker and the cupbearer), but reinstated the innocent man just as quickly.
2. He didn't react in anger when the magicians and wise men were unable to interpret his dreams. (King Nebuchadnezzar wanted to kill his wise men when they couldn't repeat his dreams (Daniel 2:12).)
3. He surrounded himself with trustworthy men with whom he had an open relationship.
4. He took counsel from his cupbearer though he was only a servant.
5. He was willing to listen to advice from a lowly Hebrew prisoner.
6. Though polytheistic himself, he respected the power of Joseph's God.
7. He looked beyond Joseph's past and recognized his character.

Imagine if Joseph had to apply for this position and how most prospective employers would view him. He was unwanted by his family, lower-class, uneducated by Egyptian standards, a slave, convicted of attempted rape, and as a Hebrew, considered to be inferior (if not subhuman).

📖 Now read Genesis 41:40–44 and describe the position and power granted to Joseph by Pharaoh.

_____

_____

_____

Do we serve an amazing God, or what? From pasture to pit, from pit to prison, from prison to prime minister! Picture Joseph's astonishment when Pharaoh advised him of his new job; not only would he be virtually running the nation, he was showered with wealth and honor.

According to verse 44 no one in all the land could raise his _____ or _____ without Joseph's permission. The magnitude of the power and authority given to him is hard to even grasp! He could have done almost *anything* he wanted to do—even retaliate. Joseph had spent thirteen years as a slave and a falsely accused prisoner. The final two years in captivity were spent in hopes of being released, but the cupbearer had forgotten him. Tormented by his siblings, kidnapped, nearly murdered, sold as a slave, wrongfully incriminated, forgotten in jail—now that was a recipe for self-pity and revenge. Most of us would have harbored bitterness, hurt, and anger; but Joseph didn't. He had it within his power to wreak vengeance on Potiphar and his wife and the cupbearer, and to vindicate himself; but he didn't. Joseph was learning what it meant to forgive, and that would serve him well in the years to come.

📖 Read Romans 12:19–21.

What are God's instructions for us concerning vengeance and retribution?

_____

_____

What do you do when you have the opportunity to get back at someone who has wronged you?

_____

_____

_____

📖 Read Genesis 41:45, 50–52.

What was Joseph's new Egyptian name?

_____

_____

What was Joseph's wife's name?

_____

_____

What were Joseph's sons' names?

_____

_____

The exact meaning of Joseph's Egyptian name is not known, though some scholars believe it means "The God Speaks and Lives." To the Egyptians it no doubt had a pagan implication, but to Joseph, each time he was called by his new name he was giving testimony to the Lord. His wife, Asenath, was the daughter of a priest and chosen for him by Pharaoh. Her name means "Belonging to the Goddess Neith." Within seven years, Manasseh and Ephraim were born to Asenath and Joseph. Do you remember the meanings of their names? *Manasseh* means "causing to forget" and *Ephraim* means "double fruit." Joseph worked for a pagan man, lived in a pagan nation, and was given a pagan wife, and yet he openly honored the Lord in the naming of his sons.

> **"So Pharaoh said to Joseph, "Since God has informed you of all this, there is no one so discerning and wise as you are."**
>
> **Genesis 41:39**

> **Oh, that we would live our lives in such a way others could recognize the Spirit of God in us!**

Earlier we discussed the importance of names to the Hebrew people, and in Week Four we saw the significance of Manasseh's and Ephraim's names. God had brought Joseph through discouragement, misery, weariness, trouble, and depression, but he felt doubly blessed. Verse 51 says God caused Joseph to forget *"all my trouble and all my father's household."* The Hebrew word translated "forget" (*nashah*) means "to neglect, remit, remove." It doesn't mean Joseph didn't remember the trials he'd gone through or that he had a family back in Canaan; it meant he had removed the anger, bitterness, and resentment from his life and was focused on the blessings God had given him.

I love this part of the account, for I believe it marks in Joseph a stage of maturity many people never achieve. He had grown from his past hurts and trials, but he didn't complain and hang on to them and let them control his life.

📖 Read Philippians 3:13, 14. The apostle Paul had the same attitude Joseph had. He didn't focus on what had happened in the past; he pressed *"on toward the goal for the prize of the upward call of God in Christ Jesus."*

🛑 APPLY Are you hanging on to bitterness, anger, or resentment from past sorrows or offenses?

_____

_____

_____

Is there someone you need to forgive?

_____

_____

_____

Life at the Top

DAY FIVE

FOR ME TO FOLLOW GOD

Pray this verse: *"Open my eyes, that I may behold Wonderful things from Your law."* (Psalm 119:18)

At the beginning of this week's study, we likened Joseph's life to a roller coaster—hills and dips, twists and turns, thrills and fear. A real roller coaster ride lasts a few minutes—you get off, catch your breath, and it's over. Real life is much different.

Some of you are trying hard to follow God, but past sins keep coming back to trouble you, and victorious living seems a long way off. Unfortunately, there are natural consequences to sin that can be long-lasting; sometimes there's nothing you can do about that aspect of it. But you don't have to live with guilt, shame, fear, and condemnation, for Christ's death, burial, and resurrection have delivered you. Satan is our enemy, and he loves to keep bringing up the past and throwing it in our faces. But remember—Jesus is your Advocate standing before the Father (1 John 2:1, 2), and Satan, the accuser, will be cast down (Revelation 12:10).

📖 Read Psalm 103:1–12.

How many of your sins have been forgiven (v. 3)?

_____

_____

With what does the Lord crown you (v. 4)?

_____

_____

With what does He satisfy you (v. 5)?

_____

_____

What does He do for the oppressed (v. 6)?

_____

_____

Fill in the blanks from verse 8: _"The LORD is _____ and
_____, _____ to _____ and
_____ in loving_____."_

What do verses 10 and 11 mean to you?

_____

_____

_____

How has God dealt with your sins (v. 12)?

_____

_____

God has forgiven all your sins; He has redeemed your life; He crowns you
with compassion and loving-kindness; He is slow to anger; He does not deal
with you according to your sins; He has removed your sins as far as the east
is from the west.

Please read that last sentence one more time and let it sink into your heart.
God has forgiven you; but have you forgiven yourself? You may be throwing your sins back into your own face; you may be the one who can't let go
of the past. Perhaps there are those who don't want you to forget, because
you offended them in some way, and they want you to pay with guilt. If
you've asked them to forgive you and tried to make things right between
you, then let it go. You can't make another person forgive you; you can only
ask forgiveness from that person and from the Lord.

Don't Waste Your Past
One reason I believe that the Bible is such a great book is because through
it the past is not wasted. Let me explain what I mean. For hundreds of years
people have been reading within its pages the stories of those who failed
miserably, as well as those who lived honorably before the Lord. Within our

*Joseph didn't wallow
in what could have
been, he found joy
and contentment in
what was.*

own study over the past few weeks we've seen the failings of Abraham, Isaac, Jacob, Joseph's brothers, Potiphar's wife, and even King David.

We've also seen some of those same people step out in faith and do great things for God. Now let me ask you some questions. Did you learn something from each of those people? Did you learn from their mistakes? Were you encouraged by their faith? Has Joseph given you some insight into godly living? If you answered yes to those questions, their past has not been wasted, nor has yours.

God doesn't want us to *live* in the past, but He does want us to *learn* from it. If you have made mistakes (and we all have), don't waste them; use what went before to show others why they should not make the same wrong choices; show them how God forgives and heals and pardons and shows His loving-kindness. There is nothing the Enemy would like better than for you to wallow in the sins of long ago, because then you will be rendered ineffective for the Lord. Why not use what you've learned to help others? I don't mean give the grimy details of sin—that's not necessary, nor is it helpful. However, when someone has experienced a situation similar to yours, extend God's love and grace and forgiveness to them as it was extended to you.

APPLY Can you think of a trial or event from your past you might use to comfort or encourage someone going through a similar situation? Briefly explain.

_____

_____

_____

_____

📖 Read 2 Corinthians 1:2–7.

What is one purpose for which God comforts us (vv. 3, 4)?

_____

_____

_____

When we share in _____, we can share in _____ (v.7).

None of us enjoys suffering (certainly Joseph didn't), but think of the multitudes facing trials who have found hope and courage from reading Genesis 37–50. I doubt Joseph was thinking at the time, *Wow, praise the Lord, my story is going to be written down to encourage others; I'm so excited to be a prisoner in this dungeon.* But, can you imagine how our attitudes about our trials would change if we could view them from God's perspective? We truly would be able to say, *"Consider it all joy, my brethren, when you encounter various trials, knowing that the testing of your faith produces endurance"* (James 1:2, 3).

According to Philippians 1:12–14, how did Paul view his trials?

_____

_____

Making an Impact for Eternity

 APPLY Do you think your life is making an impact for eternity? Why or why not?

_____

_____

_____

When we view the end result, Joseph's life was and is clearly making an impact for eternity. His position as vizier eventually saved the lives of thousands of people and paved the way for the children of Israel to become the great nation God had promised Abraham. We can see purpose in his trials and tribulations; everything makes sense in retrospect. In comparison, your life may seem less remarkable, and you can't imagine that you are making any kind of impact for eternity. But, it's all in perspective.

If you think your life has little impact, just ask:

- the mother who was at her wits' end after an exhausting week with toddlers; you volunteered to watch her child in the nursery so she could have an hour to worship her Lord.
- the missionary barely making ends meet on the mission field; you gave up your specialty coffee in order to give a little more in the offering.
- the lady who had a horrible week at work and hadn't wanted to come to church; you gave her a hug and told her you were glad she came.
- the woman who was ready to give up on her marriage; you invited her over for coffee and listened as she poured out her heart.
- the pastor who was feeling as if his whole ministry had been for naught; you baked a loaf of bread for his family and wrote a note telling him how much his sermons mean to you.
- the person who trusted Christ as Savior and will now spend eternity with Him because you took time to share the gospel.

Yes, it's all in _perspective_. When you notice the hurts of others and make yourself available to meet their needs, you are doing for them what Joseph did for Potiphar, the baker and cupbearer, Pharaoh, and his own brothers. _You_ are being Jesus to those people.

📖 In closing, please read Colossians 3:1–4.

 Dear Heavenly Father, Thank You that You have forgiven all my sins and have cast them as far as the east is from the west. Thank You that Jesus is my Advocate and that He defends me when Satan tries to bring up the past. Help me to use my past in a positive way to help others who are struggling with similar issues. Give me wisdom as I seek to bear the burdens of those who are weighted down with more than they can bear. Help me to always direct them back to You. Father, help me to see my life from Your perspective and to know that the things I do for You really do count for eternity. In Jesus' name, amen.

Let go of the past, walk in the present, let God hold the future.

Notes

7

The Real Test of Character

*J*oseph had finally made it to the top—a prestigious job, the respect of his boss and peers, wealth, community standing, political power, a socially placed (and probably pretty) wife, and two fine sons. But is that what "making it to the top" really means—financial security, a nice home, social status, a stable family? I think if we could ask Joseph, he would say he was just as much at the top as a slave in Potiphar's home and as a prisoner in a dungeon as he was as one of the most powerful men in the world, for he was a man of faith (Hebrews 11:22) and honored God whether his position was lofty or low.

Joseph had an enviable life by many standards. It would appear his problems were finally over, and he could live out his life in relative ease. Ah—*relative* ease! Those pesky relatives were getting ready to enter the scene once again, and the real test of Joseph's character was about to begin.

I'M IN CHARGE OF WHAT? HELP, LORD!

Pray this verse: *"Open my eyes, that I may behold Wonderful things from Your law."* (Psalm 119:18)

Have you ever taken a stress test? I don't mean a cardiac stress test, but the kind where you answer questions about taxing situations in your life. You get a certain number of points for each event you've recently experienced, such as a death, divorce, loss of a job, and so on, and your stress level is then measured by the number of points you accumulate. If we could add up the points for the changes and events in Joseph's life, his stress level would be off the chart. As if he hadn't experienced enough upheaval in his first thirteen years in Egypt, he now had a new job, home, wife, and family. To top it off, an entire country and nearby nations were depending on him for their very lives.

Yes, Pharaoh had put Joseph in charge, but now Joseph *really* needed God's help. Would he have the administrative skills to win these people over and lead them in this enormous undertaking? Could he overcome the racial barrier and gain their respect? Let's take a look at the responsibilities that fell to Joseph during the seven years of plenty and the subsequent famine.

📖 Read Genesis 41:33–36, 46–49, 53–57; 47:13–26.

What were Joseph's initial responsibilities (41:34, 35)?

_____

_____

_____

What percentage of the grain was stored as surplus for the famine (41:34)?

_____

_____

How old was Joseph when he became vizier of Egypt (41:46)?

_____

_____

How far did he travel in fulfilling his responsibilities (41:46)?

_____

Who was affected by the famine (47:13)?

_____

_____

_____

How did the people pay for grain (47:14)?

_____

_____

Joseph needed God's help and direction as he developed the administrative skills needed to fulfill his new responsibilities.

How did they pay for grain when their money was gone (47:15–17)?

_____

_____

How did they pay for grain when their livestock were gone (47:18, 19)?

_____

_____

What group was allowed to keep their property (47:22)?

_____

_____

Describe the system Joseph implemented so the people could have grain and provide for their families (47:23, 24).

_____

_____

_____

What was the attitude of the people toward Joseph (47:25)?

_____

_____

Only God could have prompted Pharaoh to promote a man like Joseph, with no political experience and a questionable background, because the post of vizier was difficult and stressful even without the problems of a famine. Although he had lived in Egypt for thirteen years, to the general populace he was still a foreigner, a former slave, and an ex-convict. To make matters worse, his entire plan was based on his "supposed" interpretation of the king's dreams given to him by a God they didn't even recognize. He was asking an entire nation to change their lifestyle and future plans based, from their perspective, on his word alone. With all he was up against, his accomplishments were truly amazing for that day and age.

As part of his job, Joseph had to calculate the amount of grain produced and consumed in Egypt; estimate population growth; determine where to store the grain; appoint honest and wise men to facilitate the work; train and organize the workers; and keep accurate records. He had to hire farmers and harvesters, overseers, accountants, guards, and construction workers to build granaries. He had to be an exceptional administrator, be a good judge of character, practice diplomacy, and implement a national food program that would save 20 percent for future needs. When the famine finally began, he had to deal with economic failure, immigration issues, and an increase in crime. And, when the people finally exhausted their personal supply of food and turned to the government, Joseph had to execute a program that allowed for personal responsibility without creating a crippling government welfare system.

Overwhelming, isn't it? Do you think Joseph did this amazing work on his own? Absolutely not! For along with the meanings of Pharaoh's dreams, God had given him a plan and the strength and wisdom to carry it out. Can

Only God could have prompted Pharaoh to promote a man like Joseph, with no political experience and a questionable background, because the post of vizier was difficult and stressful even without the problems of a famine.

Egypt was a massive country, and as a hands-on leader, Joseph traveled throughout the land to supervise preparations for the famine. Most of the cities were located along the Nile River and its tributaries, so he likely traveled primarily by boat.

> **"The steps of a good man are ordered by the LORD, And He delights in his way."**
>
> **Psalm 37:23 (NKJV)**

you see how God had been preparing Joseph for all those years? His life was a progression—each step of his caravan's journey being led by God to put the next step in order, the next trial, the next victory.

Let's look at the progression of Joseph's caravan. In each section below write what you think he learned during that particular period of his life that prepared him for the next stage. (If you're doing this study in a group setting, please take a few minutes to share your answers. I think you will get some interesting input from the others, because this is an area where each of you will view Joseph's life from a different perspective.)

How did Joseph's childhood and adolescence (shepherd, favored son, blended family, etc.) prepare him for slavery, leadership, and moral purity?

_____

_____

_____

_____

How did slavery prepare him for prison, teach him humility, and show him how to see to the needs of others?

_____

_____

_____

How did prison prepare him for the position of vizier, acknowledging God before pagans, and mass organization?

_____

_____

_____

_____

It was as if Joseph filed away each experience while building upon each act of faith and developing the character he needed for the next step in his journey. Wouldn't it be wonderful if we could see our own lives from that perspective—if we could trust that the Lord is working everything out for our good and His purpose?

Living with Worry and Stress
I tend to worry and fret—in other words, I stress. In fact, whenever I am reading Joseph's story and take in all he had to accomplish, I worry and stress *for him.*

 What about you? Circle the number below that represents where you are on the "worry scale."

Never worry   0   1   2   3   4   5   6   7   8   9   10   Always worry

Most people that worry don't want to be worriers; they know it's bad for their physical, mental, and spiritual health, but don't seem to be able to get it under control. The Lord tells us not to be stressed or anxious, so whether you circled zero or ten, or somewhere in between, let's look at the advice He has to give us. I've given you a number of verses to look up because worry and stress have reached epidemic levels in our society.

📖 After each of the following references, write a personal application.

Psalm 18:6

_____

_____

_____

Psalm 37:25

_____

_____

_____

Psalm 42:5

_____

_____

_____

Psalm 55:22

_____

_____

_____

Matthew 11:28–30

_____

_____

_____

Luke 12:22–29

_____

_____

_____

Philippians 4:6, 7

_____

_____

_____

"Don't tell me that worry doesn't do any good. I know better. The things I worry about don't happen."

Source unknown

> ### "Those who love Your law have great peace, And nothing causes them to stumble."
>
> ### Psalm 119:165

Hebrews 4:16

_____

_____

_____

1 Peter 5:6, 7

_____

_____

_____

Joseph was a slave who became a leader, to become a slave.

I believe there is a place for healthy concern. We should care about those who have not accepted Christ as their Savior, those who are suffering and/or in need, our government leaders, the sin in our lives. Those things should drive us to prayer and to help when we can, but we should not let worry and anxiety control our lives. Can you imagine how much less stressful our lives would be if we _really_ believed that the Lord was guiding each step of our caravan and that He was using the events of our lives to prepare us for the next work He wants us to do? I don't know what concerns may be giving you stress and anxiety, but I do know that God will give you the strength and wisdom to fulfill His purpose in you.

Joseph's road to the top was paved with a painful childhood, the pit, the auction block, slavery, betrayal, and prison. But each experience, each trial, prepared him for the next step in his journey. As an obedient slave, Joseph learned to be a leader; as an obedient leader, he learned to be a slave. When we began this Bible study, I said Joseph's life is often viewed from an overall perspective— the favored son, the dreamer, the slave, the prisoner, the vizier—Joseph in a nutshell, but we often miss the nut. I hope by this point in our study you are beginning to see the meat of the nut.

The Real Test of Character

DAY TWO

THE MEASURE OF SUCCESS: GOD DOESN'T USE A YARDSTICK

Pray this verse: _"Open my eyes, that I may behold Wonderful things from Your law."_ (Psalm 119:18)

How do you measure success? Is it based on salary, employment, social standing? Is it membership in the right club, acceptance at a prestigious school, driving a classy car, wearing stylish clothes, or knowing influential people? Is it "bigger, better, more, promotion, achievement, numbers, money, power, victory"—words often synonymous with success?

Joseph had been on his way to becoming a success back in Canaan; his father was grooming him to become the patriarch of the family, and his future prosperity was assured. Of course, there had been the difficulties of sibling rivalry, but the family had become wealthy and was growing—twelve sons and a daughter. With numbers like that, they were on their way to becoming the nation God had promised Abraham. But everything changed for Joseph when he went to look for his brothers in Shechem and was sold to the Midianites—any thoughts of success vanished. For how could slavery be considered a success in anyone's book? Wasn't it actually a huge demotion? After all, how much lower could a person get? Joseph owned nothing and had no hope for freedom—his future wasn't just bleak, it was virtually non-existent. He was destined to live out his days as nothing more than a piece of property.

Consider this. If Joseph's story had ended with slavery in Potiphar's home, would you have considered him to be a success? Explain your answer.

_____

_____

_____

Let's take it one step further, or rather, one step down. What if Joseph's story had ended with him in prison—would you have considered him to be a success then? Again, explain your answer.

_____

_____

_____

Probably, most of you answered yes to both—you would call Joseph a success in both situations. But, were your answers influenced by the fact that you know the end of his story; because you know he eventually rose to a prominent position?

_____

_____

_____

Let me ask you one more question. Do you consider *yourself* to be a success at this point in your life? Why, or why not?

_____

_____

_____

_____

(If you are doing the study in a group, please discuss your answers to the last questions.)

It's easier for many of us to see success in others than in ourselves. Why? It's because we tend to minimize our own accomplishments. On the other hand, you may be discouraged because you are doing the very things Joseph did—trying to honor the Lord, be a good example to others, resist temptation, bear the burdens of others—but you don't feel as if God is blessing or exalting you. You may see Joseph's rise to the top as a Cinderella story—instead of from servant girl to princess, from slave boy to prime minister. But for you, there is no castle in sight.

> *"For My thoughts are not your thoughts, Nor are your ways My ways," declares the LORD.*
>
> *Isaiah 55:8*

The problem is that we tend to view success differently than God does. I personally wrestle with this on a regular basis. My husband and I have been in ministry for more than thirty years, most of that time serving in small churches. We've tried to be faithful and do the right thing, but we've not seen significant numerical growth. Does that mean our years of ministry have been unsuccessful? Does it mean God is not pleased with us? No, it doesn't. But to be honest, sometimes I feel that way. Then I have to remind myself God does not use the same measuring stick I use.

📖 The following passages speak of success or prosperity. After each verse write the biblical implications for seeking and achieving success.

Genesis 39:3, 23

_____

_____

_____

Joshua 1:7, 8

_____

_____

_____

Matthew 23:11, 12

_____

_____

_____

Philippians 2:3, 4, 15, 16

_____

_____

_____

1 Timothy 6:6–12

_____

_____

_____

James 4:6

_____

_____

_____

According to the previous passages, God is seeking those who are loyal, faithful, and humble, those who serve, obey His statutes, and exalt others above themselves. If you are doing these things, in God's eyes you are a success no matter your social status, your employment, or the size of your bank account.

Becoming vizier of Egypt was a great achievement, and Joseph's subsequent acts in that position were extraordinary—he was a success. But, he was equally successful as a shepherd, a slave, and a prisoner, because success is not just found in the final accomplishment or position, it is found in the *process* that brings you to that achievement.

Look carefully at Romans 12:1, 2 once more: *"I urge you therefore, brethren, by the mercies of God, to present your bodies a living and holy sacrifice, acceptable to God, which is your spiritual service of worship. And do not be conformed to this world, but be transformed by the renewing of your mind, that you may prove what the will of God is, that which is good and acceptable and perfect."*

Joseph definitely fulfilled the first part of that verse. Whatever situation he found himself in he presented himself as a living and holy sacrifice to the Lord. Now look at verse 2. If you recall, the Greek word for "transformed" is the word from which we get our word *metamorphosis,* the amazing process by which a caterpillar turns into a butterfly. Both the caterpillar and the butterfly have a unique beauty, but the actual metamorphosis is the amazing part—the *process* of change. Joseph showed leadership and other godly qualities as vizier, but the way he conducted himself prior to that was the truly remarkable part.

Let me explain what I mean. Where we end up and what we achieve can be wonderful things, but, the *process* (our metamorphosis) of how we become men and women of obedience and godly character is the real measure of greatness. It was the *process* Joseph went through: responding to each difficult trial and disappointment; proclaiming Jehovah as the one true God; resisting temptation and keeping himself pure; putting the needs of others ahead of his own—these were the things that brought the Lord glory and honor.

Joseph never dreamed he would be a slave in Egypt, but when he found himself in that position, he became the best slave in Potiphar's home. His success as overseer was not in the position, but in how he handled himself through the *process* getting there. Though he didn't expect to end up in jail, he conducted himself as a model prisoner and looked out for the needs of others. The subsequent success in being promoted to prison manager was a manifestation of how he handled himself through the difficult *process*. When he was called before the throne to interpret Pharaoh's dreams, he came in humility and honored the Lord. The promotion to vizier was a great honor, but the *process* that got him there was what mattered.

Your life is in the *process*. The Lord may very well want you in a position of leadership, financial prosperity, or social prominence at some point, but will you be content if He chooses to take your caravan on a path that appears more ordinary to the world? Will you honor and glorify Him through your metamorphosis by obedience, uprightness, and faith? If we could only understand that we are no different from Joseph; it's simply that God is leading our caravans along different paths.

 Do you struggle with accepting God's view of success as opposed to the world's view? Spend a few minutes thinking back over the previous day's events.

> ## "I have learned to be content in whatever circumstances I am."
> ## Philippians 4:11b

- Did you encourage someone with a kind word?

- Did you help to bear the burden of someone whose load was heavy?

- Did you humbly acknowledge a mistake?

- Did you resist temptation or flee from evil?

- Did you put the needs of someone else before your own?

- Did you acknowledge God in the course of your pursuits?

- Did you honor the Lord by obeying His statutes?

- Did you show respect to those in authority over you?

Briefly describe each situation to which you answered yes.

_____

_____

_____

_____

_____

If you answered yes to any of the questions above, you are a success, and you are bringing honor and glory to the Lord through your metamorphosis.

As we close out the day, here is some food for thought. Have you ever stopped to think that as successful as Joseph was, he was never really free—he was always a slave? It's true. Even in the exalted position of vizier of Egypt with an entire nation at his command, he was still Pharaoh's slave. He couldn't go back to Canaan and live with his family, and he couldn't choose a different job. He didn't even get to choose his own wife! But Joseph was in good company and so are you, for remember, *"The Son of Man did not come to be served, but to serve . . ."* (Matthew 20:28a). That is where real success lies.

The Real Test of Character

DAY THREE

THE SHOCK OF JOSEPH'S LIFE!

Pray this verse: *"Open my eyes, that I may behold Wonderful things from Your law."* (Psalm 119:18)

In five short chapters of Genesis, we've covered a lot of ground. Approximately twenty-one years have passed since Joseph headed to Egypt with the Midianite caravan. It has been a wild ride, and it isn't over yet. Ready or not, the past is just about to catch up with Jacob and his other eleven sons.

As you read today's Scripture, you're going to be on the edge of your seat. Please read Genesis 42, then keep your Bible open as we study the passage together.

Can anyone doubt God has a sense of humor? Genesis 42 could have easily started with verse 2, but God chose to insert Jacob's comment to his sons in verse 1: *"Why are you staring at one another?"* Picture this scene: all eleven sons sitting around the tents while their food supply dwindles, and none making a move to do anything until Jacob tells them to get off their camel-hair stools and go to Egypt.

According to Genesis 42:4, why did Jacob keep Benjamin in Canaan?

_____

_____

_____

What do you think motivated Jacob's decision?

_____

_____

_____

It seems Jacob had transferred his intense fatherly affection to Benjamin after Joseph's apparent demise. Obviously, he hadn't learned his lesson on the dangers of parental partiality.

Egypt: Take One

The brothers had a long walk to Egypt. What do you think they discussed on their journey?

_____

_____

_____

I would love to have heard those conversations, or at least know what they were thinking as they trekked the same ground Joseph did so many years before; as they passed trade caravans and observed how the slaves were treated. Did they furtively glance about city streets and marketplaces searching for the familiar, now older, face of their brother—dreading, yet perhaps hoping for, a chance encounter? Little did they know an encounter was about to happen, and it wasn't by chance, but by divine design.

As a hands-on vizier, Joseph was personally involved in the sale of grain, even to those who came from foreign lands. He knew the famine had reached as far as Canaan and at some point his family might come to buy food. In twenty-one years, he must have rehearsed a thousand possible scenarios he would have with his brothers if he ever saw them again. Now, those very men bowed before him and asked to buy the grain that would save their lives. Joseph's power was perhaps never greater than at that moment.

Do you recall the word study we did on Day Four of Week Two on the word translated "bow," "bowing," and "bowed"? The Hebrew word, *shachah,* means "to prostrate oneself," as if to pay homage to royalty or God. Compare Genesis 42:6 with Genesis 37:7. The Hebrew word translated "bowed down" in both verses is exactly the same.

📖 Now, hold that thought and read Genesis 42:10.

How did Joseph's brothers address him?

_____

_____

Here the Hebrew word translated "lord" ('adown) means "sovereign" or "controller." Joseph's dreams had become a reality, and the interpretation was clear, at last. The brothers were *bowing* in obeisance to their brother, who had become a *sovereign ruler*.

What do you think went through Joseph's mind when he recognized his brothers and remembered his dreams?

_____

_____

_____

Why didn't the brothers recognize Joseph?

_____

_____

After twenty-one years, there would have been marked physical changes in all the men—now they ranged in age from their late thirties to late forties. However, Joseph would have changed most of all. In the Egyptian fashion, he would have been clean-shaven, dressed in linen, wearing eye makeup and a wig, speaking the Egyptian language, and called by a foreign name. And, they never would have expected to see their brother ruling in a foreign land.

Reading Genesis 42:7–16, I can picture each man grasping for words, trying to be heard above the others, denying the allegation they were spies, while Joseph, in semi-shock, repeated his accusation through an interpreter, desperately trying to put his thoughts in order. As he listened to his brothers' denials, what information did he learn that he so badly wanted to know (v. 13)?

_____

_____

_____

When Joseph was forced to leave Canaan, his father had been 108 years old and was now nearing 130. Many times, Joseph must have wondered if Jacob was still alive and how Benjamin had fared among the brothers who had so cruelly mistreated him. It must have taken all his will power not to reveal himself at that moment. What ultimatum did Joseph give his brothers (vv. 14–16)?

_____

_____

_____

Joseph placed his brothers in prison while they pondered his offer to bring Benjamin to Egypt. He used those three days to devise a plan that would guarantee their return with Benjamin and show if they had made genuine changes in their character.

Whom did Joseph say he feared (v. 18)?

_____

_____

For Joseph to make an accusation of espionage was plausible. The widespread famine would likely invite scrutiny from other nations hoping to steal food or launch an attack during a national crisis.

Confusion must have been added to the brothers' terror when Joseph said he feared God. Who was this strange Egyptian? Was he mocking their Lord? Why would a high-placed Egyptian official who worshipped many gods claim to reverence *their* God?

What was the brothers' reaction to Joseph's new plan (vv. 21, 22)?

_____

_____

_____

How did Joseph react to his brothers' words (v. 24)?

_____

_____

Which brother did he confine in prison (v. 24)?

_____

_____

Do you see any attitude changes in Joseph's brothers?

_____

_____

_____

Word Study

FEAR

The Hebrew word translated "fear" (*yare'*) in Genesis 42 means "to be reverent."

The brothers were in agreement as to why they were in their present state— God was punishing them for their sin against Joseph; they were reaping what they had sown (Galatians 6:7). Joseph had been distressed; now they were distressed. Joseph had pled with them; now they were pleading with this "stranger." For more than twenty years, they had tried to cover their deed, but the guilt of unconfessed sin had been a heavy burden to bear.

Read Psalm 51:1–10, then fill in the blanks for verse 10: "_____ in me a _____ heart, O God, And _____ a _____ spirit within me."

According to Psalm 38:3–10, what are the physical and emotional consequences of sin?

_____

_____

_____

_____

Until we acknowledge to God our sin, there will always be heaviness in our spirit, for only He can make us clean again, and lift the burden.

APPLY Is there sin from your past (or present) you have not acknowledged? Do you long for a clean heart? Take a few moments now to write out a prayer of confession so you can hear joy and gladness, and heal your broken bones.

_____

_____

_____

As Joseph surreptitiously listened to his brothers, he could see a change had begun to take place in their hearts; though they still had a long way to go, they were finally taking responsibility for their actions. Hearing Reuben's protests must have been particularly touching, and perhaps influenced him in choosing to keep Simeon (the second oldest) in Egypt. The whole scene proved too much for him, however, and he turned away and wept. With his emotions running high, he must have wondered if they would abandon another brother, or if they would return with Benjamin. Would he ever see his father again? With those questions unanswered, Joseph sent his brothers back to Canaan with grain for their households, provisions for the journey, and their silver secretly restored in their grain sacks.

How did the brothers and Jacob react when they found the money in their sacks (Genesis 42:27, 28, 35)?

_____

_____

_____

A simple shopping trip to Egypt had turned into a nightmare: a brother in prison, fear and trembling over finding silver in their sacks, and Jacob refusing to let them return with Benjamin.

You have to admire Reuben for coming forth with integrity and offering his own sons as collateral for Benjamin, but Jacob wouldn't let go. More than twenty years before, he had sent Joseph on a mission, and his beloved son had not returned; he was not going to take any chances a similar fate might befall Benjamin. What problems or dangers do you see in Jacob's overprotection of Benjamin?

_____

_____

_____

I think most parents can identify with Jacob; we want to do all we can to protect our children from harm. But Benjamin was a grown man with ten sons of his own (Genesis 46:21). There comes a time when we must let go and allow our children to make their own choices and decisions, for both their sakes and ours. We are not in control of their lives—God is. We have to trust He loves them even more than we do.

📖 Look at Genesis 42:38 once more. Jacob said Joseph was dead and Benjamin was left alone. How do you think this made his other ten sons feel?

_____

_____

_____

Jacob just didn't get it, did he? God blessed him with twelve wonderful sons and a daughter, but he invested his love and affection in only two. He forfeited years of blessed relationships, helped create bitterness and resentment among his children, and deeply hurt those closest to him.

APPLY Are you missing out on God's richest blessing in your relationships because your words and actions have been partial to some and insensitive to or neglectful of others? Do you try to control and manipulate the lives of those close to you? Take a few moments to prayerfully consider your relationships and ask God to show you the changes you need to make.

EGYPT: TAKE TWO

Pray this verse: *"Open my eyes, that I may behold Wonderful things from Your law."* (Psalm 119:18)

Y ou wouldn't think the drama could get any more intense, but it does. Join me in reading Genesis 43.

The famine grew worse, but in typical Jacob fashion, he ignored the problem until the last possible moment, as if the problem of Simeon and Benjamin would go away on its own. I wonder if he ever considered that he was depriving Simeon's wife and six sons (Genesis 46:10) of their husband and father.

Who finally took control of the problem (Genesis 43:3)?

_____

_____

_____

What did Judah say to convince Jacob to let them take Benjamin to Egypt (vv. 8–10)?

_____

_____

_____

This portion of Scripture marks a decided change in the character of Jacob's sons, for they finally begin to think of others ahead of themselves. First, Reuben offered his sons as surety, and then Judah, the mastermind behind the plot to sell Joseph, persuaded Jacob to allow Benjamin to go to Egypt by offering himself as a guarantee. Presumably, Judah represented the consensus of them all, for throughout the rest of the story he takes the leadership and speaks for the entire group.

Another point that suggests a change of heart is that there was nothing to stop the brothers from taking *any* young man to Joseph and presenting him as Benjamin. They could have taken one of their hired hands and no one would be the wiser; Benjamin would be safe at home and dad could rest easy. To their credit, they would not return to Egypt without the genuine article.

Arriving in Egypt, they went straight to find Joseph and were presented with another surprise—an invitation to lunch. That had to be the longest morning any of them had ever experienced. Joseph could hardly wait to spend time with Benjamin and get news of his aged father, but his brothers were terrified as to why they were dining in his home. Whether motivated by fear or integrity, they immediately offered to return the silver that was found in their bags. How did the steward respond to the brothers (v. 23)?

_____

_____

What does it tell you that the steward twice referred to God?

_____

_____

_____

I think Joseph was a godly influence on those with whom he lived and worked, and the steward's acknowledgement of God bears witness to that fact.

APPLY Describe a time when you helped someone to faith in Christ by your words or actions.

_____

_____

_____

How were the brothers treated in Joseph's home?

_____

_____

_____

How did Joseph respond when he met Benjamin (vv. 29–31)?

_____

_____

_____

For the second time, we see Joseph weeping. What does that tell you about him?

_____

_____

_____

When I get to heaven, I want to ask the Lord if I can see a replay of this luncheon. Try to take in all that was happening. Simeon was brought to them after being confined, and I'll wager they all spoke at once trying to discover what had happened in both Egypt and Canaan during the intervening months. The steward treated them as honored guests—refused their money, fed their animals, and washed their feet. When Joseph was formally introduced to Benjamin, he hurried from the room without explanation, and he was probably barely in control when he finally returned to the dining room. Next, the brothers were astounded when they were seated according to their age—presumably by chance.

"There are no less than 39,917,000 different orders in which eleven individuals could have been seated!"[1] Finally, as the honored guest, Benjamin received five times the portion of the others. In spite of all the confusion, they must have been relieved this foreign official had taken a liking to their youngest sibling.

I can't help but smile when I read the last sentence of Genesis 43: *"So they feasted and drank freely with him."* The New King James Version says, *"So they drank and were merry with him."* The Hebrew word translated "drank" (*shathah*) means "to imbibe," and "were merry" (*shaker*) means "to become tipsy." The luncheon had turned into quite a party—what a different reception from the one they had on their first trip to Egypt!

Could the tension of our story become any greater? 📖 Read Genesis 44 and let's find out.

What instructions did Joseph give his steward (vv. 1, 2)?

_____

_____

What time did the brothers leave the city (v. 3)?

_____

_____

By the next day, Joseph's brothers' bags had been packed for them, and they were sent away at first light—no doubt a bit hung over from the previous day's festivities. The whole ordeal must have left them confused, but certainly relieved that the trip had turned out so well. Benjamin and Simeon were safe, their sacks were loaded with grain, and they had partied with the prime minister of Egypt in his home. Oh, the stories they would have to tell their father and their wives and children!

What hasty vow did the brothers make when confronted by the steward (v. 9)?

_____

_____

The brothers were confident the cup was not there, but once again they must have been confused and awestruck as the steward searched their sacks from the oldest brother to the youngest.

How did the brothers react when the cup was found in Benjamin's sack (v. 13)?

_____

_____

What had Jacob done when he believed Joseph to be dead (Genesis 37:34)?

_____

_____

_____

Put Yourself In Their Shoes
MAKE UP ARTIST?

Since women and men both wore makeup in ancient Egypt, Joseph probably had to reapply his makeup after he washed his face

Word Study
DIVINATION

According to the AMG Key Word Study Bible (New American Standard Bible edition, p. 67), "there was a common practice in Egypt similar to 'crystal gazing.' Joseph's gift of telling the future was no doubt associated with that, but Joseph's trust was in God, not in a silver cup."

Judah's admission of guilt may have carried a double meaning, also referring to their original sin against Joseph.

The brothers had virtually signed Benjamin's death warrant and committed their own lives to servitude. They tore their clothes in grief, a bitter reminder they had put Jacob through the very same thing twenty-two years earlier. As they made their way back to Joseph's home, between their fear and the amount of rich foods and alcohol they had consumed the previous day, they must have been physically ill.

Sadistic Payback or Wise Test?
Though to some, Joseph's testing of his brothers may seem spiteful, I believe he was testing his brothers to see if there had been a genuine change in their hearts. He was not the naive teenager who had been forced out of Canaan twenty-two years earlier; he was a thirty-nine-year-old vizier, ruling a powerful nation, and daily dealing with corrupt and deceitful men. And, frankly, that's what he knew his brothers to be based on previous experience. Until their journeys to Egypt, Joseph's last image was of them dividing twenty pieces of silver as he was carried off to slavery. As much as he cared for his family, he wasn't going to be taken in again.

When the brothers returned to the city, Joseph "graciously" proposed to keep only Benjamin as his slave, and allow the rest to return to their homes.

Judah, once again the spokesman, gives one of the most eloquent orations found in Scripture, and he obviously spoke from his heart, for he had no time to contrive a speech. How did the brothers approach Joseph (Genesis 44:14)?

_____

_____

What guilt do you think Judah was referring to in verse 16?

_____

_____

Throughout the narrative, how does Judah address Joseph (v. 16)?

_____

_____

How does he refer to himself, his brothers, and Jacob (vv. 16, 27?)

_____

_____

What do you think Judah was acknowledging in verse 27?

_____

_____

What new information did Joseph discover (v. 28)?

_____

_____

What does Judah offer (v. 33)?

_____

_____

Judah has just offered to give up his own life for that of his brother Benjamin. His attitude, and that of his brothers, was a far cry from that of the man who led the plot against Joseph and those who followed him in it. So, what made such a dramatic change in Judah? Do you remember back in Week Four Day One when I said that the insertion of Genesis 38 and the account of Judah and Tamar seemed like an odd break in the story of Joseph? I believe these Scriptures give us insight into Judah's turnaround.

📖 Read Genesis 38:7, 9–12, 26

What were the names of Judah's sons who died (vv. 7, 9)?

_____

_____

What happened to Judah's wife (v. 12)?

_____

_____

How do you think the loss of Judah's wife and two sons and the public humiliation of his sin with Tamar might have affected his understanding of what he had done to his father?

Judah experienced the devastating loss of two sons _and_ his wife. When he stood before Joseph he was speaking from the broken heart of a father who knew what it was to lose a son. He finally understood what he had put his father through. No wonder his words were so impassioned.

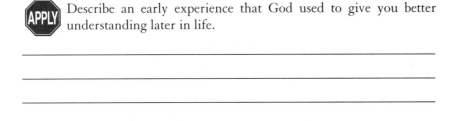 Describe an early experience that God used to give you better understanding later in life.

_____

_____

_____

_____

Joseph had amazing fortitude to sit through Judah's speech with no emotional reaction. It must have taken all his strength to once again refrain from revealing his identity, for he could see that these humble, contrite men were not the same jealous, murderous individuals he knew from childhood. Let's look at some of the changes in the men as Judah speaks for the whole group.

- They came in humility as they fell on the ground.
- They made no excuses; they simply confessed their sin before the Lord and Joseph.
- They came as servants and addressed Joseph as _lord_.
- Without malice, they acknowledged Rachel as the beloved wife.
- Without jealousy, they acknowledged Joseph and Benjamin as the beloved sons.

The brothers had already fulfilled the first dream, but the second (Genesis 37:9–11) was fulfilled as Judah referenced Jacob, though still in Canaan, as a servant to Joseph.

- They showed unconditional love and respect for their father.
- Without hesitating, Judah offered himself in exchange for Benjamin.
- They finally thought of others before themselves.

Wow! Had God been working in the lives of the brothers, or what? No doubt Joseph couldn't believe his eyes or ears. For years, he must have wondered what kind of story they had concocted to tell their father about his disappearance, and now he knew. But, that was secondary to the transformation the men standing before him had undergone.

Stopping the study right now is like leaving you hanging on a cliff, I know, but we'll resume the story tomorrow. If you can't stand the suspense, go ahead and read on.

The Real Test of Character

FOR ME TO FOLLOW GOD

Pray this verse: *"Open my eyes, that I may behold Wonderful things from Your law."* (Psalm 119:18)

This week's lessons have had it all—stress, success, shock, and shame. Joseph's life didn't get any easier, did it?

When he was promoted to vizier, every aspect of his life changed—his social and personal relationships, his job, and his all-around responsibility. Everyone wanted a piece of his time, but there are just so many hours in a day. So, how did he do it, and what can we learn from his example?

📖 Read each passage, then write its number in the blank next to the appropriate descriptions.

1. Genesis 41:34–36   _____ Personally administered workers
                           _____ Proved worthy of authority given him
2. Genesis 41:46   _____ Had an organized plan
                           _____ Kept records
3. Genesis 41:49   _____ Finished the job he started
                           _____ Didn't try to do it all himself
4. Genesis 41:54–57   _____ Humbly worked with those under him
                           _____ Chose wise men for the job
5. Genesis 47:20–26

On Day One we discussed how Joseph's administrative and organizational skills helped alleviate his job pressure and worries. We also looked at the importance of releasing our worries to the Lord. But, there is another factor that can contribute to worry, and that is lack of follow-through. Unfinished projects and tasks weigh heavily and can affect a person's ability to follow God.

 Let's do a self-evaluation and take a few lessons from Genesis. If you have any unfinished tasks or projects, please list them.

_____
_____
_____
_____

Now, prayerfully consider, and cross out anything:

- you can delegate to someone else.
- that is not your responsibility.
- that is an unnecessary time-robber or unproductive.
- you can throw away or give away.

Check your list once more. Did you eliminate everything you can? Number the remaining items in order of priority. Now, begin to complete those projects until each is finished, and only start new tasks as you have the time, need, and resources to do so.

Perhaps you're the kind of person who follows through with all your tasks and leaves nothing undone. Good. Here is a project God has for all of us: _"Bear one another's burdens, and thereby fulfill the law of Christ"_ (Galatians 6:2). We can relieve the pressures, stress, and worries of others by assisting with their burdens.

Do you know of a person or family who needs to have a load lightened?

_____
_____
_____

What can you do to help? Be specific.

_____
_____
_____

Finding True Success
Read Matthew 22:36–40.

According to Jesus, what is the greatest commandment?

_____
_____

What is the second greatest commandment?

_____
_____

Now read John 14:15.

If we love God, how will we show it?

_____
_____
_____

Based on these verses in Matthew, what do you think God considers success?

_____

_____

_____

I believe that Joseph understood that God's concept of success was not in earthly achievements, but in loving and serving God by serving others and making them prosper. It was first about a personal relationship with God, then relationships with others. I also believe Joseph knew that true success was in obedience—being where God wanted him to be, doing what God wanted him to be doing. And although that wasn't always comfortable or easy, it was always the right choice.

We sometimes think that if we follow God our lives will be relatively trouble-free, and our prayers will always be answered in the affirmative. If we experience trials and our finances are not plentiful, we assume we must be doing something wrong. If Joseph believed that to be true, he would have been an emotional and spiritual cripple. He had a difficult childhood, and then spent thirteen years in what most would consider miserable conditions with no chance of financial prosperity. Yet he was exactly where the Lord wanted him to be, doing exactly what the Lord wanted him to be doing. And, in his case, it was the unbelievers who prospered—Potiphar became wealthier; the jailer's job was made easier; and the cupbearer was reinstated to his position in Pharaoh's court. Joseph did the work, others got the blessings—but God got the glory. Joseph's entire life turned out to be that of a slave-in-training—first serving his father in Canaan, then Potiphar, next the jailer and prisoners, and finally Pharaoh in Egypt. Yet, he was a success.

Do you consider Jesus' disciples successful? Most were simple fisherman who never achieved financial success, position, or possessions, but they turned the world upside down (Acts 17:6). Was the apostle Paul a success? He spent years in jail, struggled financially, and suffered physical abuse, but he wrote most of the books of the New Testament and started numerous churches. Was Jesus successful? His public ministry lasted only three years, His own people rejected Him, and He had virtually no worldly possessions, but He changed the course of history and died for the sins of the world in obedience to the Father.

Success is not measured by what you accomplish but by who you are. Never underestimate what God can do through you in spite of your family background, race, job experience, or even failures. He did not call you to be vizier of Egypt, but you can be the best at whatever He has called you to do.

Write your own brief definition of success.

_____

_____

_____

The Lost Years

After Joseph went to Egypt, his brothers lived a lie for twenty-two years. I wonder what transpired during that time. Did they discuss Joseph's fate among themselves, or did they make a pact to never discuss it? Did they fear that one of their fellow liars would break and reveal the truth? Did they

When you understand that true success is in becoming a servant, you won't mind serving God by serving others. Remember, life on Earth is simply preparation for eternity!

ever regret their decision as they watched their father agonize in grief? Did their stomachs churn, or their faces flush, as they glanced at one another each time Joseph's name was mentioned?

Aside from Judah's story in Genesis 38, none of the brothers is mentioned again until they go to buy grain in Egypt. It's impossible to know precisely what occurred, but we can be assured God was working in their lives. Sometimes I get impatient when I don't see a quick judgment from God when people like the brothers have been so blatantly wicked. I become frustrated when I don't see a visible change in their behavior that shows they are sorry for their sin. Twenty-two years, from a human perspective, was a long time to wait for change in people, especially when their sinful behavior was so obvious, but from God's perspective, it was barely the blink of an eye. The Lord didn't tell us how He dealt with the brothers, because we don't need to know; it's not important. The only thing we need to know is He *did* deal with them, as He does with everyone, and it was according to His timetable, not Joseph's or anyone else's. Most of us want God to work speedily in the lives of others, but to be patient when it comes to disciplining us. Fortunately, He works with us as individuals and does what is uniquely appropriate to get our attention and turn us back to Him while working His purpose in our lives. Sometimes He is gentle, at other times He is more severe, but He is always loving and merciful.

📖 Read Hebrews 12:5–11.

How are we to regard God's discipline (v. 5)?

_____

_____

_____

What is the Lord's motivation for discipline (v. 6)?

_____

_____

_____

How are we to face discipline (v. 7)?

_____

_____

_____

For what purpose does God discipline us (v. 10)?

_____

_____

_____

What will discipline eventually yield (v. 11)?

_____

_____

_____

The Greek word translated "discipline" *(paideia)* means "tutorage, education, training, correction" and gives the idea of nurturing and instruction. We usually think of discipline being done out of anger or frustration because of something we did wrong, but that's not the meaning here. Though there are times we need to be punished as in verse 6 (scourging), yet the Lord always corrects or punishes us out of love, for our own good, and sometimes that involves us enduring difficult tests and trials.

 Heavenly Father, Help me to recognize the situations in my life that create stress and worry, and to rid those from my life when I can. Help me to finish the projects and tasks that I start, and not to take on more than I can handle. Show me when my view of success is more aligned with the world's view than with Yours, and may I seek success through obedience to You. Forgive me for judging others; help me leave that job up to You. Thank You for the discipline you perform in my life; help me to not despise it, but to welcome it as a manifestation of Your love for me. In Jesus' name, amen.

Works Cited

1. Henry M. Morris, *The Genesis Record* (Grand Rapids, MI: Baker Book House, 1979), 610.

Notes

Notes

8

Joseph: the Real Deal

As we come to the close of our study together, we will see what it really means to forgive and put others before ourselves; how God uses us in spite of our past failings; what to do when our expectations are not met; and the wonderful story of redemption. I can hardly wait to get started, for the drama in these final lessons is as great as we've seen so far in our study. Last week we left the brothers shaking in their sandals as Judah gave an impassioned plea to exchange his life in servitude for Benjamin's—they were willing to do anything to save their father from additional grief. God had certainly done a work in their lives, and with a little help from Joseph, they were passing the test with flying colors. They had come a long way from the murderous bunch of thugs in the fields near Dothan, and they were about to find out that Joseph was the real deal.

ME? FORGIVE YOU?

Pray this verse: *"Open my eyes, that I may behold Wonderful things from Your law."* (Psalm 119:18)

Let's get started on our reading for today. Please read Genesis 45. Sitting through Judah's oration must have been one of the most difficult things Joseph had ever done. How did he respond when Judah finished speaking (vv. 1, 2)?

_____

_____

_____

How did the brothers react when Joseph revealed himself to them (v. 3)?

_____

_____

_____

Word Study
ALIVE

The Hebrew word translated "alive" (*chay*) in Genesis 45:3 (*"Is my father still alive?"*) can also be translated "fresh" or "strong." Since Joseph already knew his father was still living, he was probably asking if Jacob would be well enough to make the journey to Egypt.

Here is another scene I want the Lord to replay for me someday. Picture the brothers, prostrate on the floor, while Judah moves forward to speak. When he finishes, Joseph sends everyone but his brothers from the room, bursts into tears, and announces he is the very brother they hated and sold into slavery. Can you see their mouths agape, silenced by shock and disbelief? The doubt then turns to guilt, terror, and utter panic.

Joseph had complete authority over his brothers' lives at this point. He could have made them slaves, imprisoned them, or even had them put to death. He could have left their wives and children to ponder their fate as they had done to Jacob when they presented him with Joseph's bloody coat. He could have made them suffer. Instead, he forgave.

Describe Joseph's plan for his family (vv. 9–11).

_____

_____

_____

Describe Pharaoh's plan for Joseph's family (vv. 16–20).

_____

_____

_____

Joseph obviously had a plan in place, and it was virtually the same as Pharaoh's. It makes me wonder if Pharaoh was privy to the unfolding drama, and had discussed it with Joseph, or if the Lord was simply working in both of their hearts. Either way, Pharaoh was so pleased with Joseph's service that he offered the brothers the best land in Egypt, housing, and gifts. He even sent carts for their wives and children. What a tribute to

Joseph's personal life and work ethic!

How did Joseph respond to his brothers' shock (vv. 14, 15)?

_____

_____

_____

I'm not so sure I would have been as gracious as Joseph. As the brothers stood speechless and trembling in fear, he immediately sought to relieve their agony. Instead of casting blame he set them free from guilt. As they rose from the floor, he didn't throw his dreams from years earlier in their faces; instead he embraced his brothers. They didn't deserve it. They didn't ask for it. But, he did it.

What do you think Joseph and his brothers discussed (v. 15)?

_____

_____

_____

This must have been a precious time of reconciliation for the brothers. Once they got over their shock, I can picture them all talking at once—Joseph asking after their families and his father; his brothers seeking the forgiveness that had already been given; each of them filling in the pieces of the missing years.

When do you think Joseph forgave his brothers? Why?

_____

_____

_____

The Scriptures do not tell us the precise time Joseph forgave his brothers. Some think it was when Judah gave his impassioned plea, others think it was at an earlier time. I'm in the latter group. I believe Joseph had come to terms with his brothers' offenses long before they made their first trip to Egypt— probably while he was still in Potiphar's household. But now, with his brothers standing before him, he had the opportunity to put action to his forgiveness.

If anyone exemplified the forgiveness of God, it was Joseph. Note below the contrasts between how his brothers had treated him and how he responded in return. If you can think of others, please add to the list.

The Brothers	Joseph
Taunted Joseph and acted cruelly	Acted kindly and reassuringly
Showed anger and bitterness	Showed love and forgiveness
Stripped him of his coat	Gave them clothing and gifts
Took him from his home	Gave them a home
Ate while he suffered in the pit	Fed them from his table
Sold him for silver	Gave them silver
Delivered him into slavery	Delivered them from the slavery of guilt
Utterly disregarded God	Acknowledged God in everything

_____

_____

_____

_____

Have you ever been so badly hurt you didn't (or don't) think you could ever forgive the person who wronged you? Maybe you have suffered long-term physical or emotional mistreatment, betrayal, rejection, desertion, or unfaithfulness in a relationship. Perhaps the scars run so deep you have never even considered forgiveness as an option, or maybe you have tried to forgive but just can't bring yourself to do it. Joseph experienced each of the aforementioned abuses at the hands of his brothers, yet he was able to forgive them, because it was what he *chose* to do.

Many years ago, a woman told some horrible, filthy lies about me; she even put her words to paper. I was angry, hurt, and embarrassed. I determined I would never forgive her, and I think I can honestly say (to my shame) I hated her. I seethed on the inside when I was around her, though I attempted to be civil on the outside. I hoped she would apologize, but because she never did I felt even more justified in my feelings. I wanted her to be hurt the way she had hurt me; I wanted her to suffer as I had suffered. I knew I was wrong, and I knew the Lord wanted me to forgive her, but I just couldn't do it. I carried that hate for several years until one day I realized I wasn't hurting her at all—I was only hurting myself. My lack of forgiveness didn't affect her, but it was eating *me* up inside. I was miserable, not her. I was allowing her to control my thoughts and emotions, and she didn't have to say a word.

I asked the Lord to forgive me for my anger and hatred and bitterness, and I forgave her. Just like that, I forgave her. She didn't ask for it, and she never said she was sorry, but I forgave anyway—for *my* sake, not hers. She didn't deserve it, and she didn't even know I did it. But *I* knew, and the burden that was lifted from me was almost physical. In fact, it probably had become physical because I had allowed it to affect me so deeply.

I don't know the details of Joseph's forgiveness of his brothers, but I've learned a few things about forgiveness from his example:

- His forgiveness was not conditional; he forgave though his brothers didn't deserve it.
- He didn't cast blame to cause guilt; he knew God could take care of that.
- He didn't make them grovel; he immediately sought to relieve their terror and agony.
- He didn't ignore there was conflict between him and his brothers.
- He used forgiveness to show them God's goodness.
- He didn't boast about his accomplishments; he gave all credit to God.
- He didn't initially trust his brothers and was careful in his dealings with them, but his forgiveness was genuine.
- He knew that God had seen the end from the beginning, even though *he* could not.

 Is there someone you have not forgiven? Stop right now and just do it. In the space on the next page, write out a prayer asking the Lord to forgive you for your anger and bitterness, then acknowledge you are forgiving the person who hurt you. It's not necessary to use names.

"Be kind to one another, tender-hearted, forgiving each other, just as God in Christ also has forgiven you."

Ephesians 4:32

"Love me when I least deserve it, because that's when I really need it."

Swedish proverb

_____

_____

_____

_____

_____

_____

When you say you can't forgive, you're saying your standard for forgiveness is higher than God's.

Joseph knew his volatile brothers well—his last instruction as he sent them on their way to Canaan was, *"Do not quarrel on the journey"* (v. 24). I can hear the conversation now.

Benjamin: "Why didn't you tell me my brother was still alive?"
Reuben: "I told you not to kill him!"
Simeon: "You guys left me in that Egyptian prison for months!"
Judah: "That was a pretty good speech I gave, wasn't it?"
All: "How in the world are we going to tell Dad what we did? I hope it doesn't kill him (and he doesn't kill us)!"

Indeed, how *did* they explain it all to Jacob? We don't know what all transpired when the brothers reached home, but after showing Jacob the wagons and all the gifts, they finally convinced him Joseph was alive. At last, he was going to be reunited with his beloved son.

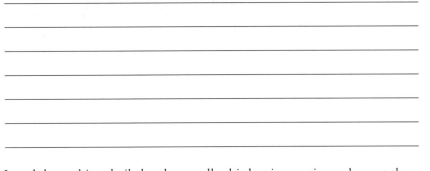

Joseph: The Real Deal

DAY TWO

GOD USES LOSERS! AND HE BLESSES THEM, TOO?

Pray this verse: *"Open my eyes, that I may behold Wonderful things from Your law."* (Psalm 119:18)

Do you ever feel like a loser when it comes to your Christian life? Perhaps I should ask the question a different way. Do you ever feel like you don't measure up to other believers, that you have failed too many times for God to use you? I think most of us have felt that way at one time or another. When you look at a life like Joseph's, it's easy to feel intimidated, to feel as if you can't live up to his standard. He was everything God would want a person to be—moral, loyal, hard-working, forgiving, a great leader, and more. It makes sense God would want to use and bless a man like him, right?

Or, perhaps you identify more with Joseph's brothers, and sometimes you feel like a loser. Looking at them, one might wonder why God would use ten men who failed so miserably. Reuben slept with one of his father's concubines; Simeon and Levi led the murderous rampage against the men at Shechem; Dan, Naphtali, Gad, and Asher had been irresponsible workers in the fields; Judah slept with his daughter-in-law; and all of them but Benjamin plotted to kill Joseph, then sold him into slavery. Then they lied and deceived for the next twenty-two years to cover their sin.

But, let's not compare ourselves to either Joseph or the brothers; rather let's see the kind of person God wants to use as we come to the final chapters of Genesis—a time of sweet reunion, new beginnings, and abundant blessings.

📖 Read Genesis 46:1–7, 26–34.

What did God confirm to Jacob at Beersheba (v. 3)?

_____

_____

_____

How many of Jacob's family moved to Egypt (vv. 26, 27)?

_____

_____

_____

Describe Jacob's reunion with Joseph (v. 29).

_____

_____

_____

God was indeed multiplying the seed of Abraham as He had promised to do. He gave His approval for Jacob's move to Egypt, and once again confirmed the covenant. As the family caravan made the journey, each step must have seemed like walking in quicksand for Jacob—he could hardly wait to see the son whom he had thought dead for so long. As for Joseph back in Egypt, the weeks of waiting were no doubt nearly more than he could bear. Every person in the procession must have rejoiced that the years of lying and deceit were finally behind them when, at last, father and son embraced.

📖 Read Genesis 47:1–12.

What was Pharaoh's gift to Jacob and his sons (v. 6)?

_____

_____

_____

When Jacob was presented to Pharaoh, what did Jacob do (vv. 7, 10)?

_____

_____

_____

How did Joseph provide for his family (vv. 11, 12)?

_____

_____

_____

Do you remember what happened when Joseph began working for Potiphar? That's right—Potiphar's household was blessed for Joseph's sake. What happened to Pharaoh and Egypt when Joseph became vizier? They were blessed for Joseph's sake. Later, on each of the brothers' visits to Egypt, Joseph blessed them by giving them abundant supplies and returning all their silver. Pharaoh then blessed Jacob and his sons by giving them the best land for their flocks, and in return, Jacob blessed Pharaoh. Finally, Joseph settled his entire family in the land with all the provisions they needed to set up and sustain their households.

Are you beginning to see a pattern? God blessed others, even unbelievers, for Joseph's sake. That is a remarkable testament to Joseph's character and attitude, and his faithfulness to the Lord. *It was more important to him that others were blessed than that he himself was blessed.* And yet, Joseph *was* blessed when those he served and loved were blessed. From my perspective, his brothers were scoundrels and didn't deserve the love, forgiveness, and gifts he bestowed on them. Even Jacob was a bit of a rascal and was unworthy of all that the Lord gave him. Fortunately, God doesn't see people from my perspective or yours. He is gracious, loving, and merciful and wants to bless us and use us even though we, too, are completely undeserving. In other words, God blesses and uses people we might call "losers."

APPLY Do you conduct yourself at work in such a way your boss wants to bless your family, too? Explain.

_____

_____

_____

Do the thoughts from today's lesson change your perspective on how God wants to use you? Explain.

_____

_____

_____

Read Romans 9:14–18.

On whom does God have mercy and compassion (v. 15)?

_____

_____

_____

Why does God choose to use certain people (v. 17)?

_____

_____

_____

Now read Isaiah 46:8–10.

We may not understand why God chooses to use certain people in specific instances; the only thing we need to know is it is by His choice, and He is using them to accomplish His purpose. He knows how to fit all the pieces

> **The fact that God blessed others, even unbelievers, for Joseph's sake is a remarkable testament to Joseph's character, attitude, and faithfulness to the Lord.**

> **"But thanks be to God, who gives us the victory through our Lord Jesus Christ. Therefore, my beloved brethren, be steadfast, immovable, always abounding in the work of the Lord, knowing that your toil is not in vain in the Lord."**
>
> **1 Corinthians 15:57**

into place; from the beginning, He knows the end. Just as Joseph and his brothers were part of God's plan to fulfill the Abrahamic covenant, He has a unique plan for you and me.

Satan would like nothing better than for you to believe you are unworthy of God's blessings, or that God won't use you because you're not as talented, gifted, or articulate as someone else, or because you have experienced failures. If that were the case, God would not be able to use anyone; we've all had failures—even Joseph.

Let's look at the kind of people God chooses to do His work. Read 1 Corinthians 1:26–31. In context, these verses show that God's message of salvation is contrary to man's natural thinking, but in the broader sense they reveal the kind of people God wants to use. Fill in the spaces according to this passage.

God has chosen to use:	God has chosen not to use:

Although Joseph was definitely wise, he was not from a noble or powerful background. As a Hebrew shepherd, he was despised and considered inferior by the Egyptians. His only notable qualifications were faithfulness and obedience—but those are the very ones for which God is looking. *"Moreover it is required in stewards that one be found faithful"* (1 Corinthians 4:2 NKJV).

Moses had a speech problem, yet he led the children of Israel out of Egypt, through the dessert for forty years, and back to the Promised Land. All the disciples abandoned, betrayed, or denied Jesus the night He was arrested in the Garden of Gethsemane, yet all but Judas spent the rest of their lives spreading the gospel throughout the world. The apostle Paul considered himself to be the worst among all sinners, yet the Lord used him to start numerous churches and write much of the New Testament.

> **"I have fought the good fight, I have finished the course, I have kept the faith."**
>
> **2 Timothy 4:7**

Have you ever thought about what you would like people to say about you at the end of your life—how you want to be remembered? I want to live my life so God blesses others because of the way I served Him. I want to be remembered as a person who had failures and disappointed the Lord many times, but finished well. I want to be a loser who was used by God to accomplish His purpose. I want to say, *"I have fought the good fight, I have finished the course, I have kept the faith"* (2 Timothy 4:7).

APPLY How would you like to be remembered?

_____

_____

_____

_____

_____

Joseph was a man greatly to be admired, and his example is one we would all do well to follow, but he was no different from you and me. He was simply a man who chose to love his Lord and be obedient to Him no matter how difficult the circumstances.

GREAT EXPECTATIONS

Pray this verse: *"Open my eyes, that I may behold Wonderful things from Your law."* (Psalm 119:18)

Have you ever considered how much of our lives we take for granted—how we expect certain things to happen and people to act a particular way? As young children, we expected our parents to love us and take care of us. As teenagers, we were filled with expectations of good health, financial prosperity, and happy relationships. As adults, our expectations may have changed somewhat but we still believe things such as: If I work, I will get a paycheck; if I raise my children according to biblical principles, they will not rebel; if I do what's right in my marriage, my spouse will always be faithful; if I'm kind to others, they will be kind in return; if people give their word, they will keep it. But our expectations are not always met—people disappoint and circumstances change, and we can't control either of those.

A few thousand years ago, Joseph and his family had the same problems. Think back through our study, then in the space below list some of the unfulfilled expectations the following people experienced.

Jacob

_____

_____

_____

Leah

_____

_____

_____

Rachel

_____

_____

_____

Reuben

_____

_____

_____

Joseph's other brothers

_____

_____

_____

Joseph

_____

_____

_____

Jacob expected to marry Rachel, but got Leah. Leah never had the depth of love she hoped to have from her husband. Rachel had to share the husband she adored, struggled with infertility, and then died giving birth to their second child. The brothers never got the love they desired from their father, and as for Joseph . . . well, this entire Bible study is evidence of *his* unfulfilled expectations, isn't it?

But before we delve into the subject further, let's get to our Scripture reading for today. It's a bit lengthy, so let's begin. Please read Genesis 47:27–50:26.

How long did Jacob live in Egypt (47:28)?

_____

_____

Jacob never expected _____ (48:11).

What special gift did Jacob give Joseph (48:22)?

_____

_____

While Joseph's life was filled with countless disappointments, he also experienced some unexpected blessings. Neither he nor Jacob thought they would ever see each other again, yet God gave them seventeen years together. After he became a slave in Egypt, he never expected to be part of his father's blessings along with his eleven brothers, let alone receive the double portion. But in the last chapter of Genesis is what I believe to be one of Joseph's greatest disappointments and unfulfilled expectations.

After Jacob died and was buried, what did the brothers fear from Joseph (50:15–18)?

_____

_____

_____

What was Joseph's emotional reaction (50:17)?

_____

_____

The adoption of Manasseh and Ephraim by Jacob made it possible for the tribes of Israel to remain at twelve while God set aside the tribe of Levi as the priestly line.

(Genesis 48:5)

Briefly recount what Joseph said to reassure his brothers (50:19–21).

_____

_____

_____

Why do you think the brothers felt Joseph might be holding a grudge?

_____

_____

_____

The brothers just didn't get it. They came to Joseph saying Jacob had asked him to forgive them, though there is no indication he said any such thing. (People usually make statements that reflect their own thinking.) Obviously, they didn't understand the concept of complete forgiveness, for they couldn't believe Joseph would not hold a grudge and try to pay them back.

As the "baby" of my family, I remember trying so hard to please my older brother and sisters, begging them to play with me, and basking in any attention they would give. I think Joseph probably experienced a similar situation and had the same desires. Instead, his brothers taunted, ridiculed, shunned, and eventually hated him. They plotted his murder, sold him into slavery, and then lied about his fate. In return, Joseph forgave and bestowed gifts upon them. He brought them to Egypt, gave them rich lands, and provided all they needed for their households. It had been thirty-nine years since the brothers threw him into the pit, and during the last seventeen years he was with them in Egypt, he did nothing but show them grace, forgiveness, and love. Is it any wonder he wept when he longed for reconciliation and they came to him with fears of retribution? Basically, Joseph had done everything right, yet his expectations of a close bond with his brothers went unfulfilled.

All of us have expectations for our relationships, churches, jobs, etc., and if we're going to be honest, from God. And, we have all experienced disappointment. The question is, How do we respond to the frustrations of unfulfilled expectations? Let's look at the reactions of Jacob's family.

As far back as Abraham we saw a pattern of deceit, control, and manipulation that was carried down through the generations. The attitude was: If things don't go your way, use others to your advantage, blame someone else, hold a grudge, run away, or murder or sell the offender(s). Eventually, there seemed to be some positive changes in the family behavior as a whole, but think of the years wasted in bitterness, anger, and resentment, and ultimately, the regrets.

APPLY Briefly describe how you handled yourself when an expectation you had was disappointingly unfulfilled.

_____

_____

_____

_____

As we've seen throughout our study, Joseph handled his unfulfilled expectations (and there were many) in a much different manner than the rest of his family did. Was he scared? Naturally. Was he angry at his brothers when they sold him? I'm sure he was. Did he ever wonder why God allowed his circumstances? Of course. Was he ever despondent? Yes. Did he cry? Oh, my, we saw Joseph weep numerous times.

So, how did he cope with those severe disappointments? He kept his focus on the truth of *who* God is—good, loving, faithful, and merciful—and he believed God had a purpose for his life in spite of his circumstances. When Joseph first revealed himself to his brothers, he told them five times (Genesis 45:5–9) God was the one who sent him to Egypt and set him up as vizier. Later, when they were fearful of revenge, he said, *"As for you, you meant evil against me,* but *God meant it for good in order to bring about this present result, to preserve many people alive"* (Genesis 50:20).

How many times have I said throughout this study God knows the end of your story just as He knew the end of Joseph's? Remember that truth. Whatever is going on in your life right now, you may be assured God will see you through the trial, no matter how difficult. Possibly you have just found out that you or a loved one has a terminal illness, or your spouse has just asked for a divorce. Maybe you've lost your job or home, or you were left out of an inheritance. Most devastating of all, perhaps you have lost a child or another loved one to death. When we don't understand the *why* we must hang on to the *what*—what we know about the *who* (God).

- He loves you – Romans 8:39.
- He is faithful – 1 Peter 4:19.
- He will never leave you – Hebrews 13:5.
- He is working all things for your good – Romans 8:28.
- He is unchanging – Hebrews 13:8.
- He is forgiving – Psalm 130:4.
- He is merciful – Psalm 145:8.
- He keeps his promises and is patient – 2 Peter 3:9.

When we don't understand the why, we must hang on to the what— what we know about the who (God).

I believe that long before he became prime minister, Joseph recognized that God had sent him to Egypt for a reason. He recognized there was purpose in his unfulfilled expectations, even though he had no idea what that purpose was. Of course, in retrospect, the whole story is clear to us. Knowing that should also give us assurance God has a purpose in *our* trials and unfulfilled expectations. When we don't understand and God has not given an explanation, we just have to trust Him. And, what a great place to be—confident, resting in the assurance God will take care of our hopes and dreams and expectations!

> *So that Christ may dwell in your hearts through faith; and that you, being rooted and grounded in love, may be able to comprehend with all the saints what is the breadth and length and height and depth, and to know the love of Christ which surpasses knowledge, that you may be filled up to all the fullness of God. Now to Him who is able to do far more abundantly beyond all that we ask or think, according to the power that works within us, to Him be the glory in the church and in Christ Jesus to all generations forever and ever. Amen.* Ephesians 3:17–21

Back to the Future

Pray this verse: *"Open my eyes, that I may behold Wonderful things from Your law."* (Psalm 119:18)

As we come to the end of Genesis, I want to go back to the future—back to Joseph's future. Eight weeks ago we began with God's promise to Abraham, which was the beginning of Joseph's future, and in a very real sense, yours and mine, too.

As we review, please list, one last time, the seven elements of the Abrahamic covenant found in Genesis 12:1–3.

_____

_____

_____

_____

In our final days together, we're going to focus on two elements of the covenant: 1) that God would make Abraham into a great nation, and 2) that all nations of the earth would be blessed through him.

In Genesis 13:14–18 God showed Abraham the land He would give to his descendants. If I had been in charge (and it's a good thing I'm not), I would have divided up that land and started Abraham, while still a young man, producing multitudes of sons and daughters to get that great nation growing. Instead, only one son of promise, Isaac, was born to Abraham and Sarah when Abraham was one hundred years old and Sarah was ninety. The next round of offspring was hardly bigger. Isaac and Rebekah had two sons, but only Jacob was chosen to carry on the covenant. When Jacob's wives began to bear children, they were finally on their way to multiplying their numbers. Then the famine came and threatened them with starvation, but God was faithful to His word and had plans bigger than they could have imagined.

According to Genesis 46:1–4, what was God's purpose in moving Jacob to Egypt?

_____

_____

_____

📖 Read Genesis 50:19, 20.

What was Joseph's part in God's plan?

_____

_____

_____

God brought Joseph to Egypt to preserve the lives of not only the Egyptians and the surrounding nations, but those of his own family. Jacob and his sons were given the best of the land, and as a result their flocks and herds grew in number. But the family grew in number as well and were eventually divided into twelve distinct tribes who became the Jewish people and the nation of Israel.

Look at the chart below and fill in the names of Jacob's twelve sons. Try to do it from memory before you look up the verses. Then do the same for Joseph's two sons.

Leah	**Bilhah**	**Zilpah**	**Rachel**
(Genesis 29:31–35; 30:17–20)	(Genesis 30:1–8)	(Genesis 30:9–13)	(Genesis 30:22–24; 35:16–18)
_____	_____	_____	_____
_____	_____	_____	_____
_____	_____	_____	_____
_____	_____	_____	_____

Joseph and Asenath
(Genesis 41:51, 52)

_____

_____

Ten of Jacob's sons plus Joseph's two sons became the twelve tribes of Israel. How did that happen when Jacob had twelve sons of his own? Jacob adopted Manasseh and Ephraim (Genesis 48:5) and through them gave Joseph the double portion traditionally reserved for the firstborn. (Remember, Reuben forfeited his right when he slept with Bilhah.) Hundreds of years later, when Moses led the Israelites out of Egypt, and they eventually divided the Promised Land under Joshua's leadership, each tribe was given an allotment.

According to Joshua 13:14, which tribe did not receive a portion of land?

_____

_____

What special responsibilities were given to the tribe of Levi (Numbers 1:47–53)?

_____

_____

The Levites became the priests for the nation of Israel, so they were not named as one of the tribes. No tribe was named specifically for Joseph—instead a tribe was named for each of his two sons. Thus, the twelve tribes of Israel were Reuben, Simeon, Judah, Issachar, Zebulun, Dan, Naphtali, Asher, Gad, Benjamin, Manasseh, and Ephraim.

When you finish this study, I would encourage you to continue reading through the Old Testament to grasp the complete significance of Joseph's captivity in Egypt. It is what allowed his family to become large in number and carry on the Abrahamic covenant. And the significance doesn't end in the Old Testament, but is ultimately fulfilled in the New Testament.

Please look back to Genesis 45:5–8.

What phrase does Joseph keep repeating to his brothers to show it was God's plan for him to be in Egypt?

_____

_____

It was *God* who sent Joseph to Egypt, not his brothers, although they were used in the process. Joseph was so convinced of that fact it changed his entire attitude about his captivity. When God directs your caravan to a specific location, you can be sure you are there for His purposes.

APPLY Describe a time when you know God placed you in a certain location or a specific circumstance for His purposes.

_____

_____

_____

_____

In the space below, I've listed some of the positive results of Joseph's suffering. Can you add to the list?

1. Fulfillment of the Abrahamic covenant continued.

2. Blessing for Israel increased, as they grew in number.

3. The world was fed.

4. God was glorified.

5. Grace and forgiveness were manifest to us for all time.

6. The message of redemption spread throughout the world.

7. _____

8. _____

9. _____

10. _____

We have listed above ways in which Joseph's captivity benefited his family and the world in general. But what about you? How has Joseph's life impacted you personally?

_____

_____

_____

_____

Although Joseph is never specifically called a "type" (figure or example) of Christ in the New Testament, many writers have noted similarities between the two. For instance, they were both rejected by their brothers, stripped of their robes, betrayed and sold for silver, unjustly accused and sentenced, and

> **When God directs your caravan to a specific location, you can be sure you are there for His purposes.**

both blessed those who persecuted them. One thing is for certain: Joseph exemplified Christ's nature throughout his life.

Think back through our study. Next to each word below, note how Jesus' nature was exhibited in Joseph's life. You can add more to the list if you wish.

Merciful

_____

Gracious

_____

Forgiving

_____

Generous

_____

Loyal

_____

Serving

_____

Compassionate

_____

Tender

_____

Considerate of others

_____

Obedient

_____

Humble

_____

Comforting

_____

_____

_____

As we close out the day, I want to share some lessons I've learned from Joseph's life that I hope will encourage you, too.

One thing is for certain: Joseph was an example of Christ's nature throughout his life.

- He didn't blame people, his upbringing, past or present circumstances, or God.
- He was content doing the job God gave to him to do.
- He served better and worked harder than anyone else around him.
- He served an unbeliever as diligently as he would a believer.
- He didn't sit back and wait for his "big break"; he gave every day his best effort.
- It was more important to him that others were blessed than that he was blessed.
- He couldn't change his circumstances, so he changed his attitude and actions.
- Though he experienced unimaginable fear, loneliness, sorrow, rejection, and despair, he never chose a detour for his caravan.
- He kept looking up though he had to keep starting over at the bottom.
- He did his best even though he didn't get paid what he was worth.
- He worked hard even though it wasn't the job he would have chosen.
- He earned his promotions through hard work.
- He was trustworthy and dependable even when no one was looking.
- He made the best of a difficult situation.
- He didn't dwell on past sorrows.
- When faced with a sinful choice, he ran.
- He did not measure success by location, circumstances, or position, but by obedience.
- He was a humble servant but he was not humiliated by his position.
- He acknowledged God in all he did and never took credit for the work God did through him.
- He was not guaranteed positive results, but he remained faithful because he knew God was faithful.
- He was more concerned others would know the name of Jehovah than in making a name for himself.
- He determined to live a godly life even when he had no hope for freedom, advancement, or a normal life of his own.
- He loved and forgave his enemies and didn't hold grudges.
- He was shrewd, faithful, and loyal with everything entrusted to him.
- He believed that *"God causes all things to work together for good to those who love God"* (Romans 8:28)—it was not just a spiritual cliché for him.

FOR ME TO FOLLOW GOD

Pray this verse: *"Open my eyes, that I may behold Wonderful things from Your law."* (Psalm 119:18)

I can hardly believe we've come to our last day together. Thank you for being faithful to do your homework and for sharing eight weeks with me studying Joseph and his family. I hope you have been as blessed as I have been.

When we began our study, I asked you to try to view Joseph's story through fresh eyes. Were you able to do that? Genesis 37–50 is sometimes presented as "just hang in there and you'll get rewards and blessings at the end of your trials," but it's so much more than that. It's about the glory God received through Joseph's testing, not about the blessings Joseph received after his testing. It's about God's love, faithfulness, protection, planning, redemption, forgiveness, healing, and blessing, not only in Joseph's life, but yours and mine as well. In 1 Corinthians 11:1 Paul writes, *"Be imitators of me, just as I also am of Christ."* In other words, as long as Paul was following Christ in obedience, the Corinthians should follow his example. The same could be said of Joseph. We can follow God by imitating Joseph's example of faith and obedience.

Today we're going to focus on the seventh element of the Abrahamic covenant found in Genesis 12:3: *"And in you all the families* [nations] *of the earth will be blessed."* While it may appear to be a generic blessing for the world, it actually has specific implications for every individual. As we read our text today, we will see why this may be the most important aspect of the covenant.

But first I want to give you the setting for the book of Galatians. A group of Jewish traditionalists called Judaizers were undermining Paul's teachings in the church at Galatia, a church he had founded on his first missionary journey (Acts 13 and 14). The Judaizers told the believers they must keep the Law of Moses in order to be saved, therefore contradicting the message of salvation by faith in Christ alone. In his letter, Paul begged the Galatians to hold to the truths he had taught them and not be swayed by false teachings.

📖 Please read Galatians 3.

How did Paul refer to the Galatians when they believed the false teachings (vv. 1, 3)?

_____

_____

_____

_____

The issue at hand was between keeping the _____ ____ _____ _____ and by hearing with _____ (v. 5).

Compare Genesis 15:6 and Galatians 3:6. How was Abraham justified?

_____

_____

_____

Who are the sons (descendants) of Abraham (v. 7)?

_____

_____

_____

Verse 8 is the key to Galatians 3 and a virtual repeat of Genesis 12:3. *"The Scripture, foreseeing that God would justify the Gentiles by faith, preached the gospel beforehand to Abraham,* saying, *'ALL THE NATIONS WILL BE BLESSED IN YOU.'"* Paul clarified the seventh element of the Abrahamic covenant—the Messiah (Jesus Christ), who would die for the sins of *both* the Jews and the Gentiles, would be descended from Abraham, who thereby became a blessing to all nations.

Those who try to keep the law are under a _____ (v. 10).

Can the law justify anyone (v. 11)? _____

How did Christ redeem us (v. 13)?

_____

_____

_____

How did the blessing of Abraham come to the Gentiles (v. 14)?

_____

_____

_____

What was the purpose of the law (vv. 19, 24)?

_____

_____

_____

Is there a law that can make us righteous (v. 21)?

_____

_____

_____

How does a person receive the promise (v. 22)?

_____

_____

_____

How do we become the children of God (v. 26)?

_____

_____

_____

There is neither Jew nor Gentile, slave nor free, male nor female, for we are all _____ in Christ Jesus (v. 28).

"And if you belong to _____, then you are _____ offspring, _____ according to _____" (v. 29 NASB 1977).

Did You Know?
THE GENTILES

The term Gentile refers to anyone who is not Jewish

Paul's frustration with the Galatians for departing from his original teachings was evident. As simply as possible, he laid it out for them (again):

- The law cannot justify anyone—even Abraham was justified by faith. (The law was given 430 years after Abraham.)

- The purpose of the law was to show us we are sinners and point us to Christ, *not* to save us.

- Trying to keep the law puts us under a curse.

- Christ's death on the cross redeems us from the curse.

- Through Christ the blessing of Abraham comes to both the Jews and the Gentiles.

- We are justified before God when we put our faith in Christ as our Savior.

Abraham lived two thousand years before Christ, so how could he be justified by Christ's death, burial, and resurrection? Verse 8 says the Scripture *foresaw* what God would do. Abraham looked *forward* to Christ's death; we look *back* to His death. For Abraham it was like a credit card—he put his faith in God and the payment was made later. For us it's like a gift certificate—the payment was made two thousand years ago and we accept it by faith now.

If you have not yet accepted God's free gift of eternal life, what is stopping you? Do you think you are too bad for God to forgive you? If Joseph, a mere man with a limited capacity for love could forgive his brothers, then surely the God of the universe, with an *unlimited* capacity for love, can forgive you.

Are you afraid to admit what you've done in the past? Joseph's brothers must have been terrified to confess their deceit and treachery to Jacob, but healing and reconciliation were the results.

Are you afraid God will keep reminding you of the past? Just as Joseph did not make his brothers grovel, nor did he throw the past in their faces, neither will the Lord bring up your past, for He forgives *completely*.

As a young girl, I tried hard to be good so I would be acceptable to God, so I could go to heaven when I died. When I was twelve years old someone showed me two Scriptures that changed my life.

"For by grace you have been saved through faith; and that not of yourselves, it is the gift of God; not as a result of works, so that no one may boast." (Ephesians 2:8, 9)

I realized I couldn't save myself by trying to do good works. Then I saw the following verse (my favorite in the entire Bible), and I discovered I could *know* I was going to heaven when I died.

"These things I have written to you who believe in the name of the Son of God [Jesus Christ]*, so that you may know that you have eternal life."* (1 John 5:13)

Joseph suffered and triumphed in Egypt so his people could flourish and eventually be a blessing to the world. Jesus suffered on the cross and triumphed through the Resurrection to fulfill the Abrahamic covenant and bring redemption to the world. If you have never accepted God's free gift of eternal life, will you do it now? Please pray with me.

Dear God, I know I'm a sinner and don't deserve Your forgiveness—yet You love me. I don't understand it all, but I do know that Jesus died on the cross to pay the sin debt I owed, was buried, and rose again. Thank you for sending Him to die for me. Right now, by faith, I am receiving Your free gift of eternal life. In Jesus' name, amen.

Heavenly Father, Thank You for sharing the life of Joseph with us. Thank You for showing me how to live a life of integrity and forgiveness, obedience and faith, trust and hope. Though I know I will sometimes fail, I want to learn from Joseph's example. I want to finish well. Thank You for dying on the cross for me. I can't repay You, and I know You don't want that, but I can use my life to serve You and others, thereby glorifying You through my life. In Jesus' name, amen.

I cannot end this study without reminding you of two things:

1. God knows the end of your story just as He knew the end of Joseph's.

2. God is directing your caravan through all the ruts, bumps, and turns.

Hang on . . . don't quit . . . finish well!

Notes

Notes

Notes

Notes

Notes

Notes

Notes

Notes

Notes